Table of Contents

CLIPP 44

College Library Information on Policy and Practice

from the College Libraries Section of the Association of College and Research Libraries

Institutional Repositories

COMPILED AND WRITTEN
BY BRIGHID M. GONZALES

Association of College and Research Libraries
A division of the American Library Association
Chicago, Illinois 2018

The paper used in this publication meets the minimum requirements of American National Standard for Information Sciences–Permanence of Paper for Printed Library Materials, ANSI Z39.48-1992. ∞

Cataloging-in-Publication data is on file with the Library of Congress.

Printed in the United States of America.

22 21 20 19 18 5 4 3 2 1

CLS CLIPP Committee

John Garrison (Chair, 2018-19; lead editor)
Westminster College
New Wilmington, Pennsylvania

Mary Francis (Chair, 2017-18)
Dakota State University
Madison, South Dakota

Jessica Brangiel
Swarthmore College
Swarthmore, Pennsylvania

Luann DeGreve
Benedictine University
Lisle, Illinois

Maya Ruscha Hobscheid
Nevada State College
Henderson, Nevada

Alyssa Koclanes
Eckerd College
St. Petersburg, Florida

Beth Daniel Lindsay
New York University Abu Dhabi
Saadiyat Island, Abu Dhabi, United Arab Emirates

Patricia Jean Mileham
Valparaiso University
Valparaiso, Indiana

Jennifer Renee Steinford
Columbia Southern University
Grand Bay, Alabama

Samantha Thompson-Franklin (secondary editor)
Lewis-Clark State College
Lewiston, Idaho

Introduction

The College Library Information on Policy and Practice (CLIPP) publishing program, under the auspices of the College Libraries Section of the Association of College and Research Libraries, provides college and small university libraries analysis and examples of library practices and procedures. This CLIPP provides information on institutional repositories (IRs) in colleges and small universities.

Traditionally the domain of large research universities seeking to capture, preserve, and make available the research output of their institutions, institutional repositories are now being initiated at small liberal arts institutions as well. Where the repositories of research universities tend to focus on the work of faculty and researchers within the institution's community and provide access to their accumulated preprints, post-prints, datasets, and other research output, the repositories at smaller institutions often feature student theses and dissertations, honors papers and capstone projects, courseware and other teaching materials, student and faculty published journals, archival materials, and other content that better reflects the teaching and student-focused missions common at smaller schools. Repositories at small schools also face unique challenges beyond the standard challenges that come with implementing an institutional repository. As colleges and small universities have begun to take part in this new form of scholarly communication, they have found new techniques and solutions unique to their size, including shifting the focus of collection to student research, joining other schools in consortiums to offset costs, creative combinations for staffing, and creating new methods for increasing faculty participation.

While there is a great deal of literature available about the development and implementation of institutional repositories in general, much of the literature focuses on large research universities or does not specifically address the challenges and strategies specific to small institutions when implementing a repository. This study focuses exclusively on institutional repositories at colleges and small universities by collecting relevant survey data about the planning, funding, staffing, and implementation of repositories at these institutions, as well as documentation on best practices, policies, guidelines, and other information germane to the deployment of an institutional repository in a non-research focused academic environment.

Literature Review and Bibliography

Introduction

In what has become one of the seminal articles on the subject, Lynch (2003) defined institutional repositories as "a set of services that a university offers to the members of its community for the management and dissemination of digital materials created by the institution and its community members" (p. 2). This definition has become widely accepted in the years since. Increasingly, institutional repositories are also associated with the open access initiative as a method of "green" open access, where authors self-archive some version of their work in open access repositories. Considering the set of services that often accompany institutional repositories, as well as their focus on the collection and dissemination of research, librarians' particular set of skills have naturally led them to take a major role in the development and implementation of IRs.

However, libraries implementing institutional repositories face major challenges, particularly at smaller institutions which are often limited in funding and available staff. While much research has been done on the subject of institutional repositories and their implementation, much of this research has focused on large institutions and research universities, as traditionally these were the institutions that were able to and interested in creating repositories. As smaller colleges and universities have started to participate and implement their own IRs, more research is needed into the best practices and guidelines for successfully implementing repositories in these smaller environments, as well as assessing the various strategies that small institutions have devised to ensure the success of their repositories.

Institutional Repositories

There are many different types of repositories, including disciplinary and subject-specific repositories, but institutional repositories in particular have been gaining in popularity since the turn of the twenty-first century. The University of Nottingham's OpenDOAR database, which tracks repositories worldwide, showed a total of just over 300 repositories in 2006. Just five years later in 2011, that number had grown to over 1,800—a 500 percent increase. Of these, 82 percent can be called institutional repositories (Cullen & Chawner, 2011). As of May 2017, there were 3,345 repositories indexed in OpenDOAR, of which 2,861 were categorized as "institutional" (University of Nottingham, 2017).

While their original purpose may have been "capturing the intellectual capital of the institution" (Rieh, Markey, Yakel, St. Jean, & Kim, 2007, p. 3), Cullen and Chawner (2011) write that this ideal is "far from an achievable reality" (p. 469). In fact, Davis & Connolly (2007) found that the majority of content in institutional repositories was made up not of the peer-reviewed research of an institution's faculty, but of gray literature and student theses. McDowell (2007) notes in her study that only 37 percent of IR content was made up of faculty scholarship, with peer-reviewed work accounting for only 13 percent. Tzoc's 2016 study of IRs at undergraduate institutions found that a number of them "used their repositories for non-IR content such as historical documents, images, videos, or artistic work" (p. 187). However, there are other valuable uses for institutional repositories, among them, continuing to "put pressure on journal publishers to allow as much free online access to their products as is economically possible" (Cullen & Chawner, 2011, p. 469).

It often naturally falls to libraries to take on the responsibility for implementing and maintaining an institution's repository, given the library's existing focus on collecting, organizing, and disseminating research and other scholarly work. Lynch and Lippincott (2005) found that for nearly 80 percent of repositories in their study the library had sole responsibility for its operation. This can place a burden on libraries, particularly financially, as they are often responsible not just for the cost of the repository itself but also for the cost of staff to maintain and run the repository.

Funding can be handled in a variety of ways. For instance, an IR can be funded as part of "the library's routine operating costs, by a special initiative supported by the library, a regular line item in the library's budget, or a grant awarded by an external source" (Markey, St. Jean, Rieh, Yakel & Kim, 2008, p. 166). However it is funded, the often substantial cost of operating an IR can be a burden, particularly for small colleges and universities which often do not have an equally substantial budget to devote to it.

Besides staffing, one of the biggest expenses of operating an IR can be the software itself. There are a wide variety of commercial and open-source platforms currently used to host institutional repositories throughout the world, including DSpace, bepress Digital Commons, EPrints, Fedora Commons, Islandora, Hydra, and others.

There are generally three different technological approaches to implementing an institutional repository: "using open source software, purchasing a commercial product, and developing an in-house system" (Rieh, St. Jean, Yakel, Markey, & Kim, 2008, p. 177). These options have various advantages and requirements that must be considered when choosing which platform to use. Some important considerations include how much the software costs, both upfront and long-term, the amount of customization available, and the potential ease of operation. Some open-source software is free; however, the cost to either hire for or outsource its setup may be substantial. Other commercial platforms may have a substantial cost upfront but include technical assistance or hosting services that would otherwise cost a significant amount.

Lynch and Lippincott (2005) found that DSpace was the dominant software package used in repositories but that there were also "a lot of locally developed systems and use of various content management packages" (Types of Materials para. 1). McDowell (2007) reported that 94 percent of the repositories in her study used either DSpace or Digital Commons. Wang (2011) also found that "the majority of the repositories worldwide were created using the DSpace platform" (p. 82). However, Markey et al. (2008) found that specifically at master's- and baccalaureate-level institutions, there was much more variety in the choice of platform than at research level institutions.

While DSpace, an open-source software platform, remains a top choice overall, Tzoc's (2016) recent study of undergraduate institutions in the U.S. found 67 with a working IR and an overall preference for bepress Digital Commons software, perhaps attributable to smaller institutions' focus on "out-of-the-box and affordable platform" (p. 187) options. Tzoc reports that the most wished-for features in a software platform by the undergraduate institutions in his study consisted of altmetrics, web management, author pages, and multimedia support. Tzoc also found that 82 percent of the undergraduate institutions in his study did not yet have an IR, concluding that future plans for implementing an IR at these institutions would likely depend on "which IR platform can develop and offer an affordable and sustainable business model for institutions with few or no technical staff; the possibility/feasibility of multi-institutional or consortium license options; or potential partnerships between mid-sized/large institutions and small institutions" (p. 190).

Several articles in the professional literature offer comparisons of the various software options, as well as strategies and criteria for readers to compare platforms based on their own needs. Corbett, Ghaphery, Work, and Byrd (2016) compare a locally hosted, open-source system such as DSpace or Fedora with a hosted, proprietary system such as Digital Commons. In the case study of Virginia Commonwealth University, the authors describe how the loss of a library staff member with expertise in DSpace, as well as their desire for the library to take part in publishing endeavors, prompted their switch from the open-source DSpace to the proprietary bepress Digital Commons platform. While the authors lament the lack of direct database access and the necessary reliance on the vendor for reports, system backups, and setting up new collections, they express satisfaction with the vendor support provided by bepress as well as the marketing and outreach features of the platform.

The authors also present the case of Northeastern University, which moved in the opposite direction, from a hosted bepress repository to their own local repository built using the open-source Fedora platform. In the case of Northeastern, the authors found that the level of customization afforded by the open-source software better suited their needs but emphasized that they had the necessary staff to maintain the software long-term—a full-time employee devoted to the management of the repository as well as half of the senior web developer's time—compared with the minimal staff needed to manage the Digital Commons repository—"0.25 FTE of the scholarly communication librarian's position and a minimal amount of time (fewer than five hours per week total, on average) from two metadata staff" (2016, p. 8).

Other available articles in the literature comparing repository platforms include Castagné (2013), who offers a point-by-point comparison of several major repository platforms, and UNESCO's Institutional Repository Software Comparison, written by Bankier and Gleason (2014). Castagné compares DSpace, EPrints, Digital Commons, and Fedora Commons across a variety of elements, including an overview of each platform, installation/administration, metadata, interoperability, content management, file format, statistics, user interface, and support. Bankier and Gleason's comparison includes Digital Commons, DSpace, EPrints, Fedora, and Islandora, and compares many of the same elements covered by Castagné, as well as additional elements such as publication tools, multimedia, social features, authentication, and accessibility.

Benefits for Small Institutions

Institutional repositories can offer a wealth of benefits to the institutions that instate them, making them a worthwhile consideration even for many small colleges and universities. While IRs have traditionally been the domain of large research universities, in recent years small institutions have begun to implement their own IRs as well. Professional literature on the topic discusses the myriad benefits of an IR to the institution, including: an increased dissemination of the institution's research output; increased access to and visibility of faculty research, the preservation of research, records, and other institutional documents; marketing for the university; hosting for open-educational resources; and participation in new forms of publishing.

Institutional repositories provide universities with a way to widely disseminate the research output of the university, from both faculty and students, by offering open access to work that was often only previously available through paid journal subscriptions. This is a benefit that often appeals to faculty members depositing their work in the IR. Davis and Connolly (2007) write that participating faculty members "cited the dissemination of research results, visibility, and the author's exposure" (Survey of Scholars para. 1) as incentives for depositing their work. Since articles in an institutional repository are often indexed in major search engines such as Google, depositing one's work in the IR can open it up to viewing by anyone, anywhere. Many platform vendors also provide search engine optimization as part of their services, which can provide "article authors with greater visibility and increased downloads, which in turn increases an author's scholarly impact" (Bruns, Knight-Davis, Corrigan, & Brantley, 2014, p. 16–17). Miller (2017) writes that "the indexing capabilities and level of detailed metadata available within IR software is what helps boost the IR items to a higher rank on the search engine result pages," and because of that, "user statistics are available to the content authors" (p. 72). This can be particularly enticing to faculty members who want to increase visibility and usage of their research.

While disciplines in the sciences have the arXiv repository and disciplines in the social sciences have the Social Science Research Network (SSRN), scholars in humanities disciplines do not have a comparable open access archive, though Davis-Kahl (2016) asserts that there are signs that the humanists are making their way toward open access as well, citing a move by the Modern Language Association (MLA) in 2012 allowing authors to retain copyright of their work, as well as new initiatives such as the Open Library of the Humanities and the Open Humanities Press. Even more recently, the MLA launched the non-profit Humanities Commons in the humanities and an independent group of scholars launched the multidisciplinary ScholarlyHub.

As more open access initiatives come onto the scholarly communications scene, proponents try to convince scholars of the personal benefits they might see from publishing in open access venues. Davis-Kahl (2016) writes of Atchinson and Bull's 2015 study of political science authors whose reliable self-archiving has led to high citation rates. As part of the effort to guide faculty toward open access publishing, Davis-Kahl asserts that "librarians must become well versed and conversant in matters of open access, copyright, and pro and con arguments," as well as "understand the scholarly habits, practices, behaviors, and priorities" of faculty (p. 152). In addition, Bruns, Brantley, and Duffin (2015) write that those librarians supporting scholarly communications should also be self-archiving their own scholarly work.

There are two philosophical views of the institutional repository: "one that views IRs as *competition* for traditional publishing, the other that sees IRs as a *supplement* to traditional publishing" (Davis & Connolly, 2007, Two Philosophical Camps para. 1). Those who view IRs as competition for traditional publishing view them as a way to take back power from journal publishers who charge scholars for access to their own work, while those who view IRs as a supplement to traditional publishing see them as a way to provide additional avenues from which to access scholarly information, including gray literature and the types of resources that are not usually widely available, such as pamphlets or bulletins. IRs were "not conceived as competition to commercial publishers, but as a resource to capture, preserve and communicate the diversity of intellectual output of an institution's faculty and researchers" (Davis and Connolly, 2007, Two Philosophical Camps para. 5). Lynch (2003) also writes that a repository's ability to host data other than scholarly works makes it "a complement and a supplement, rather than a substitute" (p. 4) for traditional scholarly publishing.

An institutional repository can also be a way to bring new research to a wide audience more quickly than traditional publishing outlets. Cullen and Chawner (2011) write that many authors find the wait from submission to publication frustrating and that researchers "found it difficult to keep up with new developments in their fields" (p. 460). The ability to deposit a pre-print of an article into an IR could make it accessible to the general public weeks or even months before publication. There is also the benefit of access to current research for researchers and scholars in developing countries that might not otherwise have access through subscription journals (Kim, 2010), as well as independent researchers not affiliated with a university.

Another commonly cited potential benefit of institutional repositories is the long-term preservation of not just scholarly research, but also university records and other institutional documents. Bruns et al. (2014) write about using Eastern Illinois University's institutional repository as a platform for "digitizing and hosting content from the University Archives" (p. 3), and how they chose "meeting minutes of faculty and staff governance committees, heavily used books and bulletins about the history of EIU, and history press releases" (p. 6–7) as some of the first collections to be developed. Davis and Connolly (2007) note as well that the original intention of DSpace was not to host purely scholarly works, but "a wide range of content types including research articles, grey literature, theses, cultural materials, scientific datasets, institutional records, and educational materials, among others" (Two Philosophical Camps para. 5).

Throughout the literature, there is discussion of the hosting of open educational resources and the opportunity to take part in new forms of publishing as potential motivation for implementing an IR. Jain, Bentley, and Oladiran (2009) in particular write about the "potential to extend the object and content of an IR beyond the 'purist' content" to "embrace classroom, and distance teaching and learning materials and offer open educational resources" (p. 3). Koopman and Kipnis (2009) add that "an institutional repository can be an excellent location to store reusable teaching materials, such as syllabi, lectures, videos, and images" (p. 115). There is also the potential for institutions to take part in new forms of academic publishing, including for libraries to essentially become publishers of their own scholarly material by using their IRs to publish and host student and faculty-led, peer-reviewed journals (Jain et al., 2009).

Finally, there is the benefit of additional marketing for the institution itself. Particularly for smaller institutions whose marketing budgets may be less robust than those of large research universities, an IR may be a way to develop interest in or drive internet traffic to the university's web presence. Jain et al. (2009) write that IRs "may be the only vehicle to attract an international audience to the institution" (p. 3), while Sheret, Walker, Beach, and Zhang (2015) write that an institutional repository can "create global visibility for an institution's scholarly research" (p. 48). Dini-Kounoudes and Zervas (2011) also mention the use of institutional repositories as "marketing tools to demonstrate faculty and student research" (p. 1), while Ferreira, Rodrigues, Baptista, and Saraiva (2008) write that an IR may "contribute to the increase of the institution's prestige" (Introduction para. 1).

In fact, the marketing benefits may extend to internal audiences as well as external, as often the institutional repository may allow libraries to work directly with and provide outreach to students and departments on campus. Exline (2016) writes that working with the undergraduate Honors Program on campus to deposit student work has shown the library how their Scholars' Repository can "make and sustain connections across the university, contribute more broadly to the teaching and research mission, and support students in their aspirations as undergraduate scholars and beyond graduation" (p. 25). Exline also writes that working with faculty or student authors "affords librarians the opportunity to discuss open access publishing, the management of intellectual property, and the assessment of research impacts" (p. 25), while Miller (2017), who advocates for collaboration with institutional departments, writes that "staff have seen an increase in student engagement since implementing the IR as a resource and practice" (p. 71).

Challenges for Small Institutions

While large research universities often have the staff and funding available to reap the many potential benefits of implementing an IR, smaller institutions face numerous challenges. Among these challenges are the focus on teaching and learning rather than research at smaller institutions, as well as fewer science faculty (Wu, 2015), the real and perceived copyright restrictions imposed by publishers (Davis & Connolly, 2007; Sheret et al., 2015; Wu, 2015), a lack of adequate staffing and/or funding (Bull & Eden, 2014; Giesecke, 2011; Wu, 2015), and the questionable sustainability of institutional repositories, financial and otherwise (Rieh et al., 2008). However, by far the most commonly cited issue that institutions of all kinds run into when implementing repositories is that of low faculty participation (Bull & Eden, 2014; Burns, Lana, & Budd, 2013; Cullen & Chawner, 2011; Davis & Connolly, 2007; Ferreira et al., 2008; Foster & Gibbons, 2005; Giesecke, 2011; Jain et al., 2009; Kim, 2010; Markey et al., 2008; Rieh et al., 2008; Sheret et al., 2015; Wu, 2015).

Lack of Faculty Participation

There has been much written in the literature about the myriad reasons for the reticence of faculty to contribute to their institutions' repositories. One of the most common reasons that faculty fail to embrace an institutional repository is that they often don't understand the potential benefits of depositing their work. Wu (2015) writes that although faculty members are often told how repositories will benefit the accessibility and publicity of their research, "most academics already operate productively within the existing methods of scholarly communication, research dissemination, and validation" (Common Challenges para. 2). Cullen and Chawner (2011) also note that "academics and researchers appear to be less likely to perceive the benefits of an institutional repository" (p. 462), and in their study found that only 24 percent had deposited their work into an IR, and the majority of those that did had only deposited one item.

Lynch and Lippincott (2005) write that "faculty need to be persuaded about the benefits" (Other Issues para. 1) of institutional repositories and assert that the most successful repositories are the ones which made systematic efforts in faculty outreach. The commonly cited benefit of increased visibility and use of their research also may not be as strong an incentive for faculty at smaller, non-research-oriented colleges and universities, since at these schools "faculty are also rewarded for excellence in teaching and service" (Markey et al., 2008, p. 168).

Even faculty members who do understand the benefits of depositing their work in a repository may be dissuaded from it by the perceived lack of prestige of depositing in an IR as compared to publishing in a traditional peer-reviewed journal. Cullen and Chawner (2011) write that the "prestige of publication venue plays the single largest role in faculty decisions about the destination of their research" (p. 462). Most current tenure and promotion systems focus on traditional scholarly publishing, and this can have an impact on how beneficial to their career faculty members perceive an IR to actually be. Kim (2010) writes that faculty members who viewed depositing their work in an institutional repository as "not harmful for their tenure and promotion were more likely to post their research work" (p. 1918) in repositories. However, he went on to write that many "seemed to hold the view that there would be little positive effect" (p. 1918), especially if it was work that was not peer-reviewed. One suggestion made by Bruns et al. (2015) is to identify the more influential faculty members of campus, particularly those who serve as journal editors or society officers, and see if they can be recruited to help communicate support for open access within their discipline.

Some faculty members also worry about plagiarism, and this concern is sometimes cited as a reason for their lack of participation. It is especially a concern for those who would post pre-prints or non-peer-reviewed work such as gray literature. Cullen and Chawner (2011), however, noted that "concerns about plagiarism seem to be waning" (p. 468–469).

Another concern that may still act as a barrier to faculty participation is the burden of the extra work and time required to self-deposit their research (Cullen and Chawner, 2011; Ferreira et al., 2008; Lynch, 2003). Kim (2010) writes that if faculty "were less concerned about additional time and effort that is required" (p. 1918), they would be more likely to self-archive their work. These findings suggest that repository staff who find ways to reduce the time commitment needed from faculty will find faculty participation less of an obstacle in creating a successful repository. Wesolek and Royster (2016) write that repositories need to be "attractive, easy, and rewarding to use" (p. 63), or even self-archiving mandates won't succeed in convincing faculty to participate. However, the authors write that once faculty have been converted to the side of open access, they "become our best ambassadors and recruiters" (p. 61).

One of the other most common faculty concerns is that of copyright, including both the real and perceived barriers created by the copyright restrictions of publishers. Wu (2015) writes that "copyright restrictions imposed by publishers will remain a key barrier for libraries to make research output publicly accessible" (Section 2.1 para. 5). However, Schwartz (2016) notes that "currently 78 percent of the publishers in the SHERPA/RoMEO database allow some type of preprint or post-print IR publishing to support open access" (p. 47).

Many times, faculty are not certain who has copyright over their work and they are often not inclined to check publishers' restrictions on posting pre- or post-prints to an institutional repository (Davis & Connolly, 2007; Ferreira et al. 2008; Kim, 2010; Sheret et al., 2015; Wu, 2015). Sheret et al. (2015) add that "many authors believe they hold copyright over their own published works when, in many cases, they do not" (p. 49).

Wu (2015) writes that "faculty are often hesitant to ask permission from publishers to deposit a work in the institutional repository" (Section 2.1 para. 4), a valuable service that could be provided by repository staff to ease the burden on faculty. Kim (2010) recommends repository staff provide copyright management services which would help address and manage "concerns about, and confusion over copyright issues" (p. 1920) that might otherwise deter faculty from participating, while Sheret et al. (2015) mention that offering copyright services has, at least for some repositories, removed a perceived burden and improved participation. Dini-Kounoudes and Zervas (2011) recommend educating faculty through help pages, user guides, and flyers as a good practice for getting faculty on board, while Scherer (2016) suggests using handouts, web-based marketing, user/author narratives, meetings and events, awards and recognition, and social media as various marketing tactics.

Another challenge faced specifically by smaller institutions is the primary focus on teaching and learning at non-research universities, which leads to overall less research output by faculty, as well as less financial prioritization given to collecting and providing access to such research. In addition, smaller colleges and universities tend to have more humanities faculty and fewer faculty members in the hard sciences who are traditionally the ones to produce the most research output and overall contribute more of their work to institutional repositories (Wu, 2015). While smaller institutions typically have more faculty in the humanities and social sciences, Wu (2015) writes that faculty in these disciplines are generally "less willing than their counterparts in the sciences to make preprints openly available to the public" (Section 2.1 para. 4), creating a barrier to building collections of faculty work for fledgling repositories.

Lack of Funding and Sustainability

Another frequent difficulty that many smaller institutions run into when starting or trying to sustain an institutional repository is a lack of funding and staff dedicated to the project (Bull & Eden, 2014; Giesecke, 2011; Wu, 2015). While one or more full-time staff may be dedicated to implementing and managing the repository at a large research university, "staff members at smaller institutions may take on repository work in addition to their normal tasks" (Nykanen, 2011, p. 15). Markey et al. (2008) also found that smaller institutions may have their library director at the helm of the institutional repository as a way to keep costs down, while Lagzian, Abrizah, and Wee (2015b) write that many of the staff responsible for an IR gain essential skills training only informally and often have to train themselves.

Institutions, large and small, have found various ways to compensate for the lack of funding, particularly in regard to funding for staff. Bull and Eden (2014) write that the lack of funding for available staff and IT resources led their institution to choose a hosted platform that would provide technical support from the vendor. Giesecke (2011) similarly writes that at the University of Nebraska-Lincoln, the lack of a computer programmer on staff led the library to choose a commercial vendor for their repository platform that would cost less per year than the salary a programmer would require.

While a lack of funding for staff can be a problem, an even bigger issue is the need for IT-knowledgeable staff in order to successfully set up and manage a repository. As Wang (2011) writes, "installation and development are certainly a big challenge for a smaller library with limited number of IT staff" (p. 84). She recommends outsourcing IT needs to a service provider as a way to reduce costs, while Rieh et al. (2008) report that using the technical support provided with a commercial repository platform reduces the need for technical staff, which may appeal to smaller institutions.

Rieh et al. (2008) go on to write that "budget and content recruitment issues" (p. 184) are the primary factors in IR sustainability, and Westell (2006) notes that "to be successful, the IR requires dedicated staffing and funding" (p. 223). Since these are the things small institutions are least likely to have in abundance, these institutions often find they must adopt a variety of strategies to ensure the success of their IRs.

Strategies for Success

As more colleges and small universities make the decision to implement their own institutional repositories, many are finding new strategies to overcome the numerous obstacles they face. Some small institutions are banding together to form or take part in consortia that pool together financial and sometimes staff resources in order to offset the often-significant costs involved in implementing an institutional repository. Lynch and Lippincott (2005) found that of those institutions that did not presently have a repository, 28 percent of universities and 21 percent of liberal arts institutions planned to use a consortium as either part or all of their strategy for implementing one, while McDowell (2007) found that over two-thirds of colleges and universities with fewer than 15,000 students participated in consortial repositories. Markey et al. (2008) also discovered that master's and baccalaureate institutions in particular were likely to use alternatives to implementing their own independent repository, "such as obtaining IR services from a consortium" or "entering into a partnership with a comparable institution" (p. 165). Xia and Opperman (2009) write that over a quarter of master's- and baccalaureate-level institutions "pooled their resources in consortia" (p. 13). Nykanen (2011) suggests that master's and baccalaureate institutions are more likely to choose a consortial repository than one for which they are wholly responsible, adding that "consortia may help ease the burden for small institutions that do not have the resources to pour into development of a repository" (p. 15).

Many smaller institutions also take advantage of the increased options in software platforms and are able to save costs by either using open-source software or turning to proprietary vendors who manage hosting and offer technical support, reducing the need for costly server space and technical staff. Nykanen (2011) writes that "a common challenge for small institutions implementing repositories is a lack of staff time and expertise, and a vendor-hosted software may be appealing for its ease of use" (p. 11). Rieh et al. (2008) add that commercial software appealed to smaller institutions in their study "because they could use technical support from the company in the absence of having local technical staff to do the job" (p. 178). Bull and Eden (2014) and Giesecke (2011) also cite the tendency of smaller institutions with limited staffing to rely on platforms that include technical support, including support that can remove the expense of keeping a full-time programmer on staff.

When selecting a software solution for an institution repository, factors to consider include the system architecture (load capability, streaming capability, security and authentication functionality, data migration (how importing or exporting content is handled, the ability for metadata harvesting), the interface(s) (how customizable is the interface and the workflow, it is mobile-enabled), metadata (what schemas are supported, how searches are handled), and content considerations (what formats can be ingested, how are version control or embargoes handled) (Simons and Richardson, 2013). Simons and Richardson cite Kott (2012) in suggesting that the current best practice for selecting or building a repository is emphasizing "extensibility and flexibility" (p. 178).

While staffing itself can be an issue for smaller institutions, many often repurpose or share staff from other service areas in the library in order to keep personnel costs low. At Humboldt State University, for example, a committee of librarians manages the digital repository along with a systems employee and a cataloger, all doing work on the repository in addition to their regular job duties (Wrenn, Mueller, & Shellhase, 2009).

Simons and Richardson (2013) write that while this type of collaboration is often necessary, it often results in repository staff who must have or acquire "some level of familiarity with domains outside their immediate areas of expertise" (p. 31). The authors specify the core knowledge categories for a successful repository implementation as specific software, copyright legislation, and knowledge of open access issues; however, they note that the majority of respondents in their study "had not been taught anything about digital repositories in the course of obtaining their degrees" (p. 50–51). To compensate, they report that the majority of their survey participants relied heavily on technical support from outside teams such as IT.

Rather than emphasizing collaborative responsibility for institutional repositories, Miner and Davis-Kahl (2012) suggest that designating one person to be responsible "signals the library's intent to fully support the repository" (p. 8–9). They point to larger institutions that tend to involve archivists in their repository development and assert that the important work of "verifying the accurate ingest and description in the repository of born-digital institutional records is a responsibility that does and should reside with the archives" (p. 8).

Bruns et al. (2014) write about a different approach in maintaining the repository at Eastern Illinois University, where a repository librarian spends just over half of their time on repository work and the rest on additional librarian duties, while their work is supplemented by the work of various student workers and staff. Schwartz (2016) writes of having a committee for the IR at Southeastern University which contained "members from every department on campus to become ambassadors and builders to encourage participation and support" (p. 44) of the program. Citing this as a method of success, he writes that faculty serving on the committee "are more likely to take ownership and individual pride in the IR and thus contribute to the scholarship it should contain" (p. 44).

With their student-centered focus on teaching and learning, colleges and small universities often align their repositories with their institution's mission, focusing on the collection and dissemination of student research rather than on the sometimes more difficult collection of faculty research. Wu (2015) writes that at master's and baccalaureate institutions, "student evaluations, curricula design, and classroom observation by academic deans carry more weight than research output in the tenure and promotion process" (Section 2.2 para. 2). As such, the traditional mission of an IR, "to collect, preserve, and provide access to the intellectual output of faculty and students" (Section 4, para. 1), may not be as enticing to faculty who see their mission as focused on teaching and learning. Instead, repositories at these institutions often focus on collections that further the missions associated with teaching and learning institutions, such as "creating and sharing teaching resources" (Section 5 para. 2). Wu recommends targeting student work as a way for "small institutions to adhere to the essential objective of IRs: to collect, preserve, and disseminate the intellectual output of an institution in digital form" (Section 2.2 para. 3). Exline (2016) also found that there was "stronger campus support and fewer barriers to collecting undergraduate research than for faculty and graduate student scholarship" (p. 16).

This appears to be a common strategy among smaller institutions. Nykanen (2011) writes that 67 percent of items in the repositories she documented were student work, including "predominantly dissertations, theses, and undergraduate honors papers and award-winning papers, essays, prose and poetry, student-created curriculum guides, and even one audio recording of an award-winning music performance" (p. 13). Nykanen writes that focusing on student work in repositories gives students the ability to permanently link to their own work in graduate applications or to show family and friends, as well as gives prospective students a better understanding of the kind of research done by students at the institution. Similarly, Rozum and Thoms (2016) write of providing students who deposit their work in Digital Commons with their own SelectedWorks site, giving them an online presence with links to their scholarship that can be used for graduate school, fellowship, or scholarship applications. In addition, depositing senior capstone projects "provides data for outcomes and assessment" that can then be used for the accreditation process (p. 316).

Xia and Opperman (2009) also found that "repositories implemented by Master's and Baccalaureate institutions tend to emphasize teaching materials and student works more than research universities" (p. 10), adding that half of the content in their study had been contributed by students. McDowell (2007) writes that a substantial percentage (41.5 percent) of repository content in all academic IRs is student-produced, while Markey et al. (2008) report that 27.3 percent of respondents in their study cited undergraduates as major contributors to their repositories. Capturing and maintaining this student scholarship can be particularly beneficial as a means to "promote the undergraduate research program, highlight opportunities for student scholars at the participating institutions, and provide evidence of the institution's dedication to supporting the efforts of students" (Rozum, Thoms, Bates, & Barandiaran, 2015, p. 804).

When it comes to collecting student work, the focus has traditionally been on theses and dissertations. Since many institutions already collect student theses and dissertations in print form, it is fairly easy for these institutions to make the digital submission of a student's work a requirement as well. Rieh et al. (2007) call theses and dissertations the "low-hanging fruit for many colleges and universities" (p. 6), and many smaller institutions implementing repositories have used this fruit "to create critical mass early and easily" (Rieh et al., 2008, p. 181). The hope is that this critical mass of content will attract the attention of faculty and encourage them to deposit their own work. Xia and Opperman (2009) write that a focus on the collection of student work helps repositories align their missions with the institution's mission of teaching and learning, something ultimately necessary for their success, while Wu (2015) notes that "despite the unique challenges they face, repositories at small academic institutions can grow as long as they prove themselves an asset in undergraduate education" (Section 6 para. 1).

One method suggested by Miller (2017) is to focus outreach on one college or department at a time. As the library partners with individual departments to add collections to the repository, "the campus becomes increasingly more aware of the IR as a resource" (p. 71). Scherer (2016) also writes that outreach cannot be left to one individual or even one unit of the library, but rather that "collaboration among various internal library partners who will advertise the repository with those they interact with the most" (p.161) is what is required for success.

Davis-Kahl, Fishel, and Hensley (2014) consider the inclusion of undergraduate work in institutional repositories to be a key method of educating students on open access issues that will potentially benefit them long after they graduate. By including topics such as "authors rights, economic factors of scholarly publishing, and open access principles" (p. 443) in required library components for first-year students, librarians "play an important role in building students' knowledge about key elements of the research lifecycle" (p. 444). Davis-Kahl (2012) writes that educating students about these topics should be a part of the mission of undergraduate education, creating graduates who can be "effective advocates for access to their own work, or for access to research that can aid them in becoming informed and critical researchers, consumers, and citizens" (p. 212).

Many smaller institutions may also focus on alternative collections such as archives. Bruns et al. (2014) write that early collections in the institutional repository at Eastern Illinois University "included meeting minutes of faculty and staff governance committees, heavily used books and bulletins about the history of EIU, and historical press releases" (p. 6-7). Koopman and Kipnis (2009) mention that digitizing archival material for the repository not only gave staff members new skills but also relieved some of the burden on the university's archivist, while Rieh et al. (2007) write that archival and manuscript collections were highly valued by both large and small institutions.

Encouraging Faculty Participation

In addition to expanding the types of content they collect, many smaller institutions are also finding new ways to encourage faculty participation. Many of the most recommended methods involve direct outreach to faculty by librarians or by other faculty members. Wu (2015) documents how the repository at Roger Williams University was populated in its early stages by sending out a periodic call for submissions to faculty, which was successful "for a number of years until responses to the calls began to wind down" (Section 3.2 para. 1). Ferreira et al. (2008) also write about directly inviting members of their community to deposit their work; however, they also found success by implementing a self-archiving policy which mandated that all work produced by members of the university be deposited in the IR. In addition, they write about offering a financial incentive to entice faculty to deposit their work, though this strategy is not commonly suggested in the professional literature. These two strategies together made up what they wrote of as the "most effective measure implemented" (Section 4 para. 2). Chant (2016) also writes that when targeting faculty for IR submissions, it helps to "tie it to things that already matter to academics, such as tracking (and increasing) citations and other proof of usage of their work" (p. 20), while Scherer (2016) suggests emphasizing the altruistic benefits of open access to motivate faculty who would prefer their work to be freely available.

While implementing a policy that mandates that faculty deposit their work in the institutional repository seems to have had the desired effect for Ferreira et al. (2008), several authors advise against using this kind of heavy-handed approach to content recruitment. Lynch (2003), for one, wrote that any institution that "requires deposit of faculty or student work and/or uses the institutional repository as a means of asserting control or ownership over these works will likely fail, and probably deserves to fail" (p. 6). Zhang, Boock, and Wirth (2015), whose university did in fact institute an open access mandate, found that faculty submissions to the IR actually declined slightly after the mandate, suggesting "that passing an OA [open access] policy alone is not a guarantee of increased faculty engagement in OA initiatives" (p. 9). In fact, institutionally mandated OA policies can make some publishers more restrictive in what they allow authors to archive. Instead, what had greater success was their previous tactic of searching Web of Science citations for new faculty publications and requesting a copy from the faculty member for deposit. By using this approach, "the percentage of authors with articles available in the IR increased almost 250% one year after the project" (p. 8-9).

Many other institutions have chosen to pursue faculty submissions by tracking down articles and offering to deposit them on faculty's behalf. Sheret et al. (2015) and Giesecke (2011) both mention tactics such as requesting faculty CVs to obtain a list of current publications or otherwise locating faculty work which they can then, with permission, deposit to the IR. Wrenn et al. (2009) go so far as to regularly search faculty and department web pages for new citations as well as set up alerts in various databases to receive notice of new publications.

Another method sometimes used is to identify a prominent faculty member who might be willing to form a strategic alliance with the library and do the recruiting among their fellow faculty. Bull and Eden (2014) and Sheret et al. (2015) both mention this tactic, with Bull and Eden writing that "faculty listen to other faculty when it comes to issues related to scholarship and research" (p. 5). Zhang et al. (2015) also suggest that "attitudes and practices of particular colleges towards OA have an impact on faculty rate of deposit" (p. 10).

Although Bull and Eden advise that librarians should not be the driving force behind the repository, others have found success by using librarian liaisons to reach out to faculty directly. Foster and Gibbons (2005) write that library liaisons meet with faculty individually to provide information about the IR's benefits, while Jain et al. (2009) also mention librarians' roles in engaging with faculty to generate content. Dini-Kounoudes and Zervas (2011), Ferreira et al. (2008), and Markey et al. (2008) all discuss offering workshops, training, and presentations, along with other targeted marketing efforts, at faculty and department meetings. Ferreira et al. (2008) disclose that they "found that sometimes the best way to reach our target audience is not to aim our discourse directly at them, but instead to flood the surrounding channels that nourish their informational needs" (The Promotional Plan para. 3).

However, the use of librarians as liaisons or advocates for open access initiatives comes with its own challenges as these subjects are not always well covered in the course of obtaining one's degree. Bruns et al. (2015) noted liaisons' concerns about practical training or that they might be considered unwelcome among academic scholars in regard to such topics. The authors write about a scholarly communication coach program in which potential liaisons are given a "toolkit" of resources to perform their duties, including information on authors' rights, checking copyright permissions, describing a data management plan, and avoiding predatory publishers. They also cite "familiarity with discipline publishers' CTAs and with the Sherpa/ROMEO tool" as key to performing these duties (p. 24).

Once faculty have been persuaded to deposit their work in the institutional repository, there are a number of features that can then be used to show value, potentially having the effect of snowballing content generation. Bruns et al. (2014) write that "upon being presented with a well-populated repository, EIU faculty responded positively" (p. 11). Many institutions also use the success of their student theses and dissertation collections to then appeal to faculty to deposit their work. Sheret et al. (2015) and Giesecke (2011) write of using automatically generated monthly download reports that are sent out to faculty as part of their recruitment efforts. Ferreira et al. (2008) also used download reports that would summarize the number of downloads as well as a top authors page. Ferreira et al. write that "these types of statistical services enabled authors to appreciate the tremendous impact that their deposits produce once the materials become available to the outside world" (Section 3.2 para. 4). Foster and Gibbons (2005) also discuss creating individual faculty researcher pages within the repository platform that "serve as a showcase for all of the researcher's work" (Enhancing the IR para. 3).

The IR as a Service

Another method of encouraging faculty and others to deposit work in an IR is to offer a variety of services to authors as part of the repository, including copyright clearance, metadata, data management services, and archiving assistance. Since creating metadata and other methods of making research discoverable falls amongst librarians' traditional skill sets, this is an area where librarians have great potential to add value, and metadata services are mentioned several times throughout the literature as a possible added service (Bull & Eden, 2014; Giesecke, 2011; Westell, 2006). Burns et al. (2013) write that "academic librarians add value to the scholarly communications process when they establish institutional repositories by, among other things, enhancing the discoverability of work through robust metadata and providing a permanent URI [Uniform Resource Identifier] for that work" (Section 2 para. 4).

Another important area is providing copyright services, including copyright clearance, advising on authors' rights, and obtaining copyright permissions. Sheret et al. (2015) write that "many faculty members do not understand copyright, the various levels of copyright clearance, or how to obtain the proper clearances. Removing this burden has lessened confusion and improved faculty participation" (p. 54). Many repositories also offer assistance with archiving faculty members' work in addition to, or instead of, self-submission, which is a service appreciated by many faculty members (Bull & Eden, 2014; Koopman & Kipnis, 2009; Rieh et al., 2008; Westell, 2006; Wrenn et al., 2009). Dini-Kounoudes and Zervas (2011) write that it is a good practice "to give them the option to use the self-archiving process or to forward their work to the Library staff and upload their work for them" (p. 2).

While there are a large variety of services that institutional repositories offer as ways to encourage more participation, Rieh et al. (2008) write that there is "little consensus among the IR staff about what they perceive and define as service components of IRs," and that in spite of the number of services on offer at various institutional repositories, that "developing a good service was not a priority for most IR staff" (p. 182).

Measuring Success

One aspect of institutional repositories that has not been thoroughly explored in the professional literature, even for repositories at large universities, is how to measure their success. What constitutes success may vary greatly depending on the repository's fundamental purpose as determined by the institution. And the measures of a successful repository at a large research university may be quite different from that of a repository run by an individual college or a consortium of small colleges.

Thibodeau (2007) writes that one might define a repository as successful "if it functions as an OAIS [Open Archival Information System] in a reliable and trustworthy manner" (Section 2 para. 2), but Lagzian, Abrizah, and Wee (2015a) cite content recruitment, services, sustained funding, and "acceptance by the target audience" (p. 198) as critical success factors. Thibodeau also considers repositories whose missions are central to that of their institution, writing that their success may also hinge "on how well it contributes to other activities within the institution" (Section 2.1 para. 7).

Others cite user download counts as the way to measure a repository's success. Rieh et al. (2008) write that "although nearly half of our respondents indicated that they employ user counts as one of the metrics to measure their IRs success, only 10 percent indicated that they have interviewed their users" (p. 174). While user and download counts are not the only way to measure success, they are certainly one of the easiest to track and one that might have the most impact on administrators, making it potentially crucial to a repository's continued survival. As Bull and Eden (2014) write, "many IRs fail to generate the necessary usage and traffic to warrant continuing long-term support and resources" (p. 15).

Bruns and Inefuku (2016) provide a number of additional metrics by which repositories can be measured, including item downloads, item uploads, the number of items in the repository, the location of the repository's visitors, the number of participating units on campus, and the number of participating faculty. Their research indicates that item downloads is the most commonly used metric for repository assessment; however, they also suggest that breaking down items into categories can help measure the university's research output as well as track compliance with open access mandates, while measuring unit or faculty participation can be "useful in targeting education and outreach activities" (p. 219). Other potentially useful metrics they mention include campus participation rates and benchmarking against previous metrics or peer institutions.

A new method of measuring success for scholarly publications that can also be applied to repositories is that of altmetrics, which measure the impact of non-traditional metrics such as social media activity like "bookmarks, online mentions and discussions, likes and shares" (Holmberg, Haustein, and Beuke, 2016, p. 236), as well as mentions and links in mainstream media and news articles. Holmberg et al. write that while it may take months or years for article citations to be counted, activity on social media is "available in real time" (p. 235). They also suggest that as social media activity becomes a more important part of the scholarly communication lifecycle, these metrics could be early indicators of citations to come; however, currently there are "no standards for collecting, aggregating, or presenting altmetrics" (p. 241).

Conclusion

Much of the literature already published focuses on large research universities, as well as on challenges that those implementing institutional repositories face, particularly in regard to faculty participation. Only a small number of publications from the past several years have started to look with a particular focus on the implementation of repositories by small, non-research universities and the unique challenges they face.

As more colleges and small universities start to implement their own institutional repositories, either through consortiums or on their own, more research focused on this specific environment is needed to document not only the particular challenges that may make implementation difficult for these institutions, but also the strategies they have used, both successfully and unsuccessfully, to implement and sustain an institutional repository. Practical, well-researched guidelines and best practices have yet to be established that would assist institutions at this level in decisions regarding their own repositories.

Also needed are consistent standards by which to measure success. There are not a great deal of guidelines for measuring success even among repositories at large research universities, but given the sometimes vast differences in purpose, and thus use, of repositories at smaller institutions, it seems that different measures may be required. Additional research, including perhaps a long-term look at the lifespan of these repositories, may be necessary to determine which have been successful and exactly what that means.

The professional literature that has been published on this topic gives smaller institutions with fledgling repositories or plans to create one a good introduction to the challenges they may face and strategies they may undertake, but they will need established best practices and guidelines supported by continued research to ensure long-term success.

References

Bankier, J. G., & Gleason, K. (2014). Institutional repository software comparison. Retrieved from http://unesdoc.unesco.org/images/0022/002271/227115e.pdf.

Bruns, T., Brantley, J. S., & Duffin, K. (2015). Scholarly communication coaching: Liaison librarians' shifting roles. Retrieved from http://thekeep.eiu.edu/lib_fac/99.

Bruns, T. and Inefuku, H. W. (2016). Purposeful metrics: Matching institutional repository metrics to purpose and audience. In B. B. Callicott, D. Scherer, & A. Wesolek (Eds.), *Making institutional repositories work* (pp. 213–234). West Lafayette, Indiana: Purdue University Press.

Bruns, T. A., Knight-Davis, S., Corrigan, E. K., & Brantley, J. S. (2014). It takes a library: Growing a robust institutional repository in two years. *Faculty Research & Creative Activity.* Paper 98. Retrieved from http://thekeep.eiu.edu/lib_fac/98.

Bull, J., & Eden, B. L. (2014). Successful scholarly communication at a small university: Integration of education, services, and an institutional repository at Valparaiso University. *College & Undergraduate Libraries, 21*(3/4), 263–278. doi:10.1080/10691316.2014.932264.

Burns, C. S., Lana, A., & Budd, J. (2013). Institutional repositories: Exploration of costs and value. *D-Lib Magazine, 19*(1/2). doi:10.1045/january2013-burns.

Castagné, M. (2013). Institutional repository software comparison: DSpace, EPrints, Digital Commons, Islandora and Hydra. *University of British Columbia.* doi:http://dx.doi.org/10.14288/1.0075768.

Chant, I. (2016). Increasing IR participation. *Library Journal, 141*(3), 20–21. Retrieved from https://www.libraryjournal.com/.

Corbett, H., Ghaphery, J., Work, L., & Byrd, S. (2016). Choosing a repository platform: Open source vs. hosted solutions. *VCU Libraries Faculty and Staff Publications.* Retrieved from http://scholarscompass.vcu.edu/libraries_pubs/33.

Cullen, R., & Chawner, B. (2011). Institutional repositories, open access, and scholarly communication: A study of conflicting paradigms. *The Journal of Academic Librarianship, 37*(6), 460–470. doi:10.1016/j.acalib.2011.07.002.

Davis, P. M., & Connolly, M. J. (2007). Institutional repositories: Evaluating the reasons for non-use of Cornell University's installation of DSpace. *D-Lib Magazine, 13*(3/4). doi:10.1045/march2007-davis.

Davis-Kahl, S. (2012). Engaging undergraduates in scholarly communication outreach, education, and advocacy. *College & Research Libraries News, 73*(4), 212–222. doi:https://doi.org/10.5860/crln.73.4.8744.

Davis-Kahl, S. (2016). Faculty self-archiving. In B. B. Callicott, D. Scherer, & A. Wesolek (Eds.), *Making institutional repositories work* (pp. 143–157). West Lafayette, Indiana: Purdue University Press.

Davis-Kahl, S., Fishel, T. A., & Hensley, M. K. (2014). Weaving the threads: Scholarly communication and information literacy. *College & Research Libraries News, 75*(8), 441–444. doi:https://doi.org/10.5860/crln.75.8.9179.

Dini-Kounoudes, A. D. & Zervas, M. (2011). Best practices and policies in institutional repositories development: The Ktisis case. *3rd International Conference on Qualitative and Quantitative Methods in Libraries.* Retrieved from http://ktisis.cut.ac.cy/handle/10488/4837.

Exline, E. (2016). Extending the institutional repository to include undergraduate research. *College & Undergraduate Libraries, 23*(1), 16–27. doi:10.1080/10691316.2014.950782.

Ferreira, M., Rodrigues, E., Baptista, A. A. & Saraiva, R. (2008). Carrots and sticks: Some ideas on how to create a successful institutional repository. *D-Lib Magazine, 14*(1). doi:10.1045/january2008-ferreira.

Foster, N. F., & Gibbons, S. (2005). Understanding faculty to improve content recruitment for institutional repositories. *D-Lib Magazine, 11*(1). doi:10.1045/january2005-foster.

Giesecke, J. (2011). Institutional repositories: Keys to success. *Journal of Library Administration, 51*(5/6), 529–542. doi:10.1080/01930826.2011.589340.

Holmberg, K., Haustein, S. & Beucke, D. (2016). Social media metrics as indicators of repository impact. In B. B. Callicott, D. Scherer, & A. Wesolek (Eds.), *Making institutional repositories work* (pp. 235–248). West Lafayette, Indiana: Purdue University Press.

Jain, P., Bentley, G., & Oladiran, M. T. (2009). The role of institutional repository in digital scholarly communications. *Proceedings of African Digital Scholarship & Curation.* Retrieved from https://www.researchgate.net/profile/Priti_Jain7/publication/237322259_The_Role_of_Institutional_Repository_in_Digital_Scholarly_Communications/links/542134480cf203f155c6164e.pdf.

Kim, J. (2010). Faculty self-archiving: Motivations and barriers. *Journal of the American Society for Information Science and Technology, 61*(9), 1909–1922. doi:10.1002/asi.21336.

Koopman, A., & Kipnis, D. (2009). Feeding the fledgling repository: Starting an institutional repository at an academic health sciences library. *Medical Reference Services Quarterly, 28*(2), 111–122. doi:10.1080/02763860902816628.

Lagzian, F., Abrizah, A., & Wee, M. C. (2015a). Critical success factors for institutional repositories implementation. *Electronic Library, 33*(2), 196–209. doi:10.1108/EL-04-2013-0058.

Lagzian, F., Abrizah, A., & Wee, M. (2015b). Measuring the gap between perceived importance and actual performance of institutional repositories. *Library & Information Science Research, 37*(2), 147–155. doi:10.1016/j.lisr.2014.06.007.

Lynch, C. A. (2003). Institutional repositories: Essential infrastructure for scholarship in the digital age. *ARL Bi-Monthly Report 226.* Retrieved from http://old.arl.org/bm~doc/br226ir.pdf.

Lynch, C. A., & Lippincott, J. K. (2005). Institutional repository deployment in the United States as of early 2005. *D-Lib Magazine, 11*(9). doi:10.1045/september2005-lynch.

Markey, K., St. Jean, B., Rieh, S. Y., Yakel, E., & Kim, J. (2008). Institutional repositories: The experience of master's and baccalaureate institutions. *portal: Libraries and the Academy, 8*(2), 157–173. doi:10.1353/pla.2008.0022.

McDowell, C. S. (2007). Evaluating institutional repository deployment in American academe since early 2005: Repositories by the numbers: Part 2. *D-Lib Magazine, 13*(9/10). Retrieved from http://www.dlib.org/dlib/september07/mcdowell/09mcdowell.html.

Miller, A. (2017). A case study in institutional repository content curation: A collaborative partner approach to preserving and sustaining digital scholarship. *Digital Library Perspectives, 33*(1), 63–76. doi:10.1108/DLP-07-2016-0026.

Miner, M., & Davis-Kahl, S. (2012). Collecting campus culture: Collaborations and collisions. *Journal of Librarianship and Scholarly Communication, 1*(2), 1–12. doi: http://doi.org/10.7710/2162-3309.1053.

Nykanen, M. (2011). Institutional repositories at small institutions in America: Some current trends. *Journal of Electronic Resources Librarianship, 23*(1), 1–19. doi:10.1080/1941126X.2011.551089.

Rieh, S. Y., Markey, K., Yakel, E., St Jean, B., & Kim, J. (2007). Perceived values and benefits of institutional repositories: A perspective of digital curation. *An International Symposium on Digital Curation*. Retrieved from http://citeseerx.ist.psu.edu/viewdoc/download?doi=10.1.1.134.3831&rep=rep1&type=pdf.

Rieh, S. Y., St. Jean, B., Yakel, E., Markey, K., & Kim, J. (2008). Perceptions and experiences of staff in the planning and implementation of institutional repositories. *Library Trends, 57*(2), 168–190. doi:10.1353/lib.0.0027.

Rozum, B., & Thoms, B. (2016). Populating your institutional repository and promoting your students: IRs and undergraduate research. In B. B. Callicott, D. Scherer, & A. Wesolek (Eds.), *Making institutional repositories work* (pp. 311–318). West Lafayette, IN: Purdue University Press.

Rozum, B., Thoms, B., Bates, S., & Barandiaran, D. (2015). We have only scratched the surface: The role of student research in institutional repositories. Retrieved from http://digitalcommons.usu.edu/cgi/viewcontent.cgi?article=1236&context=lib_pubs.

Scherer, D. (2016). Incentivizing them to come: Strategies, tools, and opportunities for marketing an institutional repository. In B. B. Callicott, D. Scherer, & A. Wesolek (Eds.), *Making institutional repositories work* (pp. 159–173). West Lafayette, Indiana: Purdue University Press.

Schwartz, N. R. (2016). Creating an institutional repository. *The Christian Librarian, 59*(1), 43–47. Retrieved from http://www.acl.org/index.cfm/publications/the-christian-librarian/.

Sheret, L., Walker, T., Beach, G., & Zhang, J. (2015). A primer on how to launch an institutional repository successfully. *Charleston Advisor, 16*(3), 48–55. doi:10.5260/chara.16.3.48.

Simons, N. & Richardson, J. (2013). *New content in digital repositories: The changing research landscape*. Oxford, U.K.: Chandos Publishing.

Thibodeau, K. (2007). If you build it, will it fly? Criteria for success in a digital repository. *Journal of Digital Information, 8*(2). Retrieved from https://journals.tdl.org/jodi/index.php/jodi/article/view/197/174.

Tzoc, E. (2016). Institutional repository software platforms at undergraduate libraries in the United States. *College & Undergraduate Libraries, 23*(2), 184–192. doi:10.1080/10691316.2014.959230.

University of Nottingham, UK. (2017, May 15). OpenDOAR—The Directory of Open Access Repositories. Retrieved from http://www.opendoar.org/find.php.

Wang, F. (2011). Building an open source institutional repository at a small law school library: Is it realistic or unattainable?. *Information Technology and Libraries, 30*(2), 81–84. doi: 10.6017/ital.v30i2.3008.

Wesolek, A & Royster, P. (2016). Open access policies: Basics and impact on content recruitment. In B. B. Callicott, D. Scherer, & A. Wesolek (Eds.), *Making institutional repositories work* (pp. 55–68). West Lafayette, Indiana: Purdue University Press.

Westell, M. (2006). Institutional repositories: Proposed indicators of success. *Library Hi Tech, 24*(2), 211–226. doi:10.1108/07378830610669583.

Wrenn, G., Mueller, C. J., & Shellhase, J. (2009). Institutional repository on a shoestring. *D-Lib Magazine, 15*(12). doi:10.1045/january2009-wrenn

Wu, M. (2015). The future of institutional repositories at small academic institutions: Analysis and insights. *D-Lib Magazine, 21*(3/4). doi:10.1045/september2015-wu.

Xia, J., & Opperman, D. B. (2010). Current trends in institutional repositories for institutions offering master's and baccalaureate degrees. *Serials Review, 36*(1), 10–18. doi:10.1016/j.serrev.2009.10.003.

Zhang, H., Boock, M., & Wirth, A. A. (2015). It takes more than a mandate: Factors that contribute to increased rates of article deposit to an institutional repository. *Journal of Librarianship and Scholarly Communication, 3*(1), eP1208. doi:10.7710/2162-3309.1208.

Analysis and Discussion of Survey Results

Introduction

The CLIPP survey on implementing institutional repositories in small or midsized academic libraries was sent to ACRL's survey list of 1,091 library directors who met these demographic criteria. After conducting a pilot survey, the final survey was sent out on November 17, 2016, and after an email reminder and an extension, closed on January 6, 2017. The survey was open for a total of seven weeks and one day. A total of 180 participants initiated the fifty-question survey, resulting in a 16.5 percent participation rate with an 85.7 percent confidence level. However, only 141 of the participants completed the survey, for a rate of 12.9 percent. This falls short of the target 95 percent confidence level, which would have required at least a 26.1 percent participation rate, so the results are not considered generalizable. However, the survey results and subsequent analysis presented here can be used as a snapshot of how some small and midsized academic libraries have planned for and implemented institutional repositories and provide a basic guideline and starting point for libraries that wish to do the same and face similar financial or staffing limitations. The full survey instrument and response rates for each question can be found in Appendix A.

The survey uses skip logic so that, after answering the initial demographic questions, if a participant indicated that they had not yet launched or made plans for a repository at their institution they would be taken to the end of the survey and given the opportunity to make open-ended comments about their plans or other considerations regarding implementation of an IR at their institution. Participants who answered that they *had* launched a repository at their institution were taken through the remainder of the survey and asked to answer questions about the planning, set up, policies, promotion, and other details about their IR. Of the 180 participants who took the survey, 58 indicated that they had launched an institutional repository and were taken through the remainder of the survey, while 91 indicated that they had either started planning but not yet launched an institutional repository or had not started planning and either did or did not plan to launch an institutional repository in the future. Thirty-one participants did not answer this question and exited without completing the survey.

Demographics

Of the 180 participants who started the survey, 26 exited the survey after providing contact information but before answering any demographic or IR-related survey questions. One hundred and fifty-four participants answered the demographic questions asked at the survey's beginning.

The first question asked for the Carnegie classification of the participant's institution. Forty-seven participants (30.5 percent) selected Bac/A&S: Baccalaureate Colleges—Arts & Sciences. Twenty participants (13.0 percent) selected Bac/Diverse: Baccalaureate Colleges—Diverse Fields. Two participants (1.3 percent) selected Bac/Assoc: Baccalaureate/Associate's Colleges. Forty-three participants (27.9 percent) selected Master's/S: Master's Colleges and Universities (smaller programs). Twenty-three participants (14.9 percent) selected Master's/M: Master's Colleges and Universities (medium programs). Nineteen participants (12.3 percent) selected Master's/L: Master's Colleges and Universities (larger programs).

Carnegie Classification	Number	Percentage
Bac/A&S	47	30.5%
Master's/S	43	27.9%
Master's/M	23	14.9%
Bac/Diverse	20	13.0%
Master's/L	19	12.3%
Bac/Assoc.	2	1.3%

Table 1: Carnegie classifications of participating institutions.

When looking at the Carnegie classification for institutions that have launched an IR the numbers vary. Twenty-four participants from institutions with an IR (41.4 percent) were from Bac/A&S: Baccalaureate Colleges—Arts & Sciences. Two participants (3.5 percent) were from Bac/Diverse: Baccalaureate Colleges—Diverse Fields. One participant (1.7 percent) was from Bac/Assoc: Baccalaureate/Associate's Colleges. Ten participants (17.2 percent) were from Master's/S: Master's Colleges and Universities (smaller programs). Ten participants (17.2 percent) were from Master's/M: Master's Colleges and Universities (medium programs). Eleven participants (19.0 percent) were from Master's/L: Master's Colleges and Universities (larger programs).

Of the institutions that indicated they have not launched an IR, twenty-two participants (24.2 percent) were from Bac/A&S: Baccalaureate Colleges—Arts & Sciences. Seventeen participants (18.7 percent) were from Bac/Diverse: Baccalaureate Colleges—Diverse Fields. One participant (1.1 percent) was from Bac/Assoc: Baccalaureate/Associate's Colleges. Thirty-two participants (35.2 percent) were from Master's/S: Master's Colleges and Universities (smaller programs). Twelve participants (13.2 percent) were from Master's/M: Master's Colleges and Universities (medium programs). Seven participants (7.7 percent) were from Master's/L: Master's Colleges and Universities (larger programs). The table below shows a comparison between the Carnegie classification of those institutions that have launched an institutional repository and those institutions that have not.

Carnegie Classification	With IR	Without IR
Bac/A&S	24	22
Master's/L	11	7
Master's/S	10	32
Master's/M	10	12
Bac/Diverse	2	17
Bac/Assoc.	1	1

Table 2: Carnegie classification of participating institutions with and without an IR.

Of the 154 participants who answered the question about Carnegie classification, only 149 went on to answer questions 10 through 12 regarding whether or not their institutions have an active IR, which accounts for the total of 149 shown in the following graph, as well as in the subsequent data comparing demographic data of institutions with and without an IR.

Participants were then asked whether they belonged to a public or private institution. One hundred and eighteen participants (76.6 percent) came from a private institution while 36 (23.4 percent) came from a public institution. For institutions that have launched an IR, 46 (79.3 percent) identify as private and 12 (20.7 percent) identify as public. For institutions that have not launched an IR, 68 (74.7 percent) identify as private and 23 (25.3 percent) identify as public.

Participants were also asked for the number of FTE students and faculty at their institutions, as well as the number of FTE librarians and library support staff. The original population of 180 participants reported a range of FTE students between 567 and 12,034, with a mean of 3,059, a median of 2,300, and a mode of 1,500. For FTE faculty, participants reported a range from 24 to 809, with a mean of 199, a median of 150, and modes of 75, 100, and 150. Participants reported a range of FTE librarians from 1 to 35, with a mean of 7.6, a median of 6 and a mode of 5. FTE library support staff showed a range from 0 to 560, with a mean of 13, a median of 6, and a mode of 1.

The institutions that have launched an IR (58) reported a range of 800 to 13,034 FTE students, with a mean of 3,639, a median of 2,582.5, and a mode of 1,500. These institutions also reported a range of 40 to 800 FTE faculty, with a mean of 256, a median of 234, and multiple modes including 75, 110, 140, 200, 250, 259, 275, 500, and 700. Institutions with an IR also reported that they employed between 2 and 28 FTE librarians, with a mean of 10, a median of 9, and a mode of 7. They also reported between 1 and 50 FTE library support staff, with a mean of 12, a median of 10, and modes of 3.5, 4, 11, and 12.

Institutions that have not launched an IR (91) reported a range of 567 to 10,000 FTE students, with a mean of 2,676, a median of 2,000, and a mode of 2,300. These institutions reported a range from 24 to 809 FTE faculty, with a mean of 165, a median of 119.5, and a mode of 100. They employed between 1 and 35 FTE librarians, with a mean of 5.8, a median of 5, and a mode of 5. They reported a range from 0 to 560 FTE library support staff, with a mean of 14, a median of 4.5, and a mode of 1.

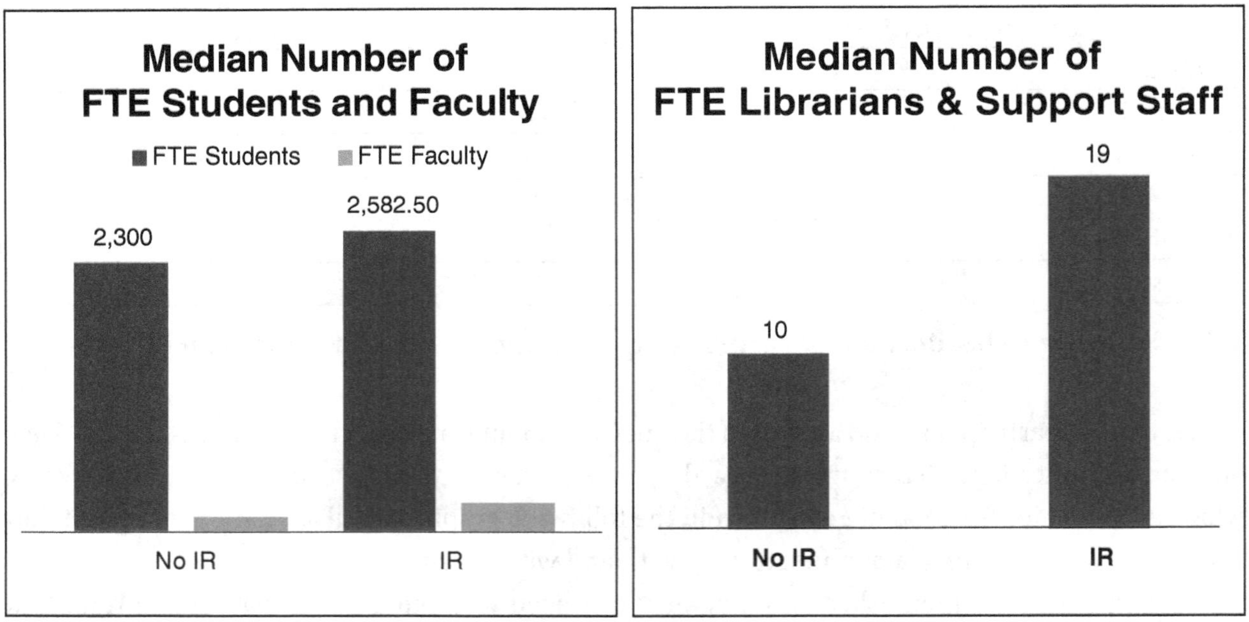

Figure 1: Median number of FTE students and faculty and the median number of FTE librarians and library support staff of institutions with and without an IR.

It is worth noting that while the numbers of FTE students is not substantially different between institutions that have launched an IR and those that haven't, the median student to faculty ratio of institutions with an IR is 11:1 whereas at institutions without an IR the median ratio is 19:1. Additionally, the median number of combined FTE librarians and library support staff for institutions with an IR is twice that of institutions without one, suggesting that institutions with fewer library staff may be less likely to implement an institutional repository.

Participants were also asked at what stage of planning and implementation their institution's repository was currently, and 149 participants answered this question. Thirty-nine (26.2 percent) answered that they had not started any planning for an IR and did not currently have plans to do so. Thirty (20.1 percent) answered that they had not started any planning for implementing an IR but had plans to do so at some point in the future. Twenty-two (14.8 percent) answered that they had started planning for the implementation of an IR but had not yet launched anything to the public. One (0.7 percent) answered that they had launched an IR but no longer actively manage or maintain it. Fifty-seven (38.3 percent) answered that they had launched and currently manage and maintain at least one IR.

Participants were also asked when their IR was made available to the public. Of the 58 participants who answered that they had previously launched an IR, six (4.03 percent) had made their IR available to the public within the last year. Fourteen (9.40 percent) had launched an IR within the last two to three years. Nineteen (12.75 percent) had launched an IR within the last four to five years. And nineteen (12.75 percent) had launched an IR more than five years ago. Of the institutions reporting they had already launched an IR, the majority (65.5 percent) had launched their IR four or more years earlier.

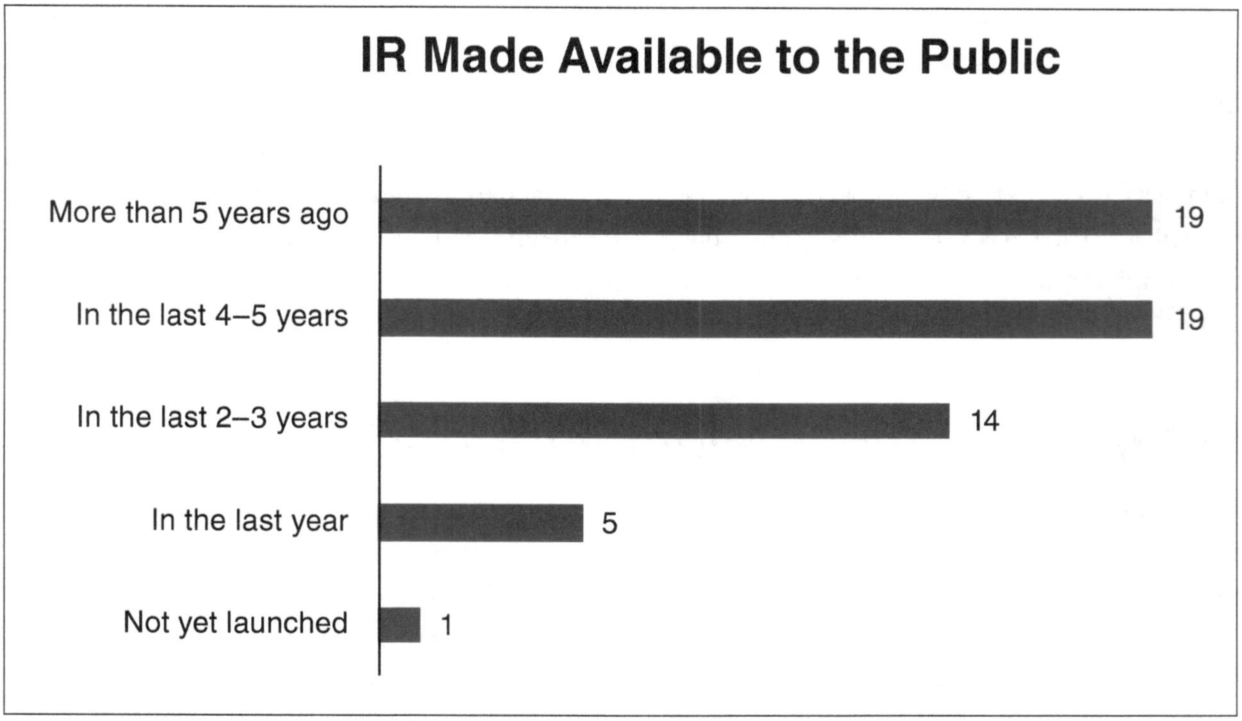

Figure 2: When participating institutions made IR available to the public.

Forty-four participants answered the question asking for the total number of items currently housed in their institutional repository, if that information was known or available. The range in the total number of items was large, with the smallest IR housing only 29 items and the largest over 72,000 items. The mean number of items was 6,568, the median was 2,455, and the mode was 1,032.

Participants were also asked to provide the total number of item views, with or without download, if that information was known or available. Twenty participants provided information for this question. The range in item views was also quite vast between libraries. Views ranged from 348 at the low end to almost six million at the high end. The mean number of item views was 446,329, the median was 10,500, and the mode was 5,094.

Finally, participants were asked to provide the total number of item downloads for the institutional repository, if that information was known or available. Thirty participants provided information for this question. The range of item downloads was also quite large with a low of zero downloads and a high of almost four million downloads. The mean number of item downloads was 706,663, the median was 281,491, and the mode was 7,389.

	Total Number of Items	Total Item Views	Total Item Downloads
Least	29	348	0
Most	72,604	5,946,557	3,927,454
Median Value	2,455	10,500	281,491

Table 3: Least, most, and median number of items, item views, and item downloads.

The remainder of the survey asked participants to provide more detail about the planning and implementation of institutional repositories in their small and midsized college and university libraries. Although 58 of the survey participants indicated that they had launched an IR at their institution, only 56 went on to complete the remainder of the survey questions. The following data was provided only by participants who confirmed that their institution currently has a repository. The survey, and subsequent analysis, has been broken down into sections on planning and implementation, staffing and personnel, policy development, and services and content development.

IR Planning and Implementation

The section of the survey on planning and implementation asked participants to answer questions about the purpose of their institution's IR, choice of software platform and the factors that went into making that decision, as well as overall costs and sources of funding.

When asked if the institution conducted a needs assessment prior to implementing the IR, the majority of participants (41 or 73.2 percent) answered that they did not, while only 15 (26.8 percent) answered that they had. However, all but one participant (55 or 98.2 percent) answered that the goals or purpose of the institutional repository directly align with all or part of the institution's mission.

When asked to identify the primary purpose of the IR, with the primary purpose being defined as the *one* main focus of collection development for the repository, the predominant response was "to collect, preserve, and disseminate all research and scholarship associated with the institution (both student and faculty)," with 32 participants (57.1 percent) selecting this option. Seven participants (12.5 percent) selected "to collect, preserve, and disseminate university records and/or archives" as the primary purpose. Six participants (10.7 percent) selected "to collect, preserve, and disseminate student research and scholarship," and three participants (5.4 percent) selected "to collect, preserve, and disseminate faculty research and scholarship" as the primary purpose. None of the participants selected either "to collect, preserve, and disseminate teaching and learning materials such as courseware, open-educational resources, and course syllabi" or "to host publications produced by the institution such as student or faculty journals." Eight participants (14.3 percent) selected "other" and indicated that their institution's repository had a primary purpose consisting equally of several or all of the options presented. Some of these wrote in specific other purposes such as "to host exhibition catalogs published by the campus gallery" or "special digital collections."

Participants were asked which software platform was used for their institutional repository, with a number of choices consisting of popular institutional repository software options, as well as the option to write in a unique selection. Several of the available software options were not selected by any of the participants, including Eprints, Fedora, Omeka, and Hydra. The most popular choice was bepress Digital Commons, with 34 participants (60.7 percent) selecting this option. Six participants (10.7 percent) selected CONTENTdm. Four participants (7.14 percent) selected DSpace (self-hosted). Three participants (5.4 percent) selected DSpace (hosted by

DuraSpace). Two participants (3.6 percent) selected in-house system, and one participant (1.8 percent) selected Islandora. Another six participants (10.7 percent) selected "other." Two of the participants who selected "other" wrote in DSpace hosted by Longsight, while another mentioned DSpace hosted by a consortium. Other write-in selections included Sobek, Ebrary's DASH, and Shared Shelf.

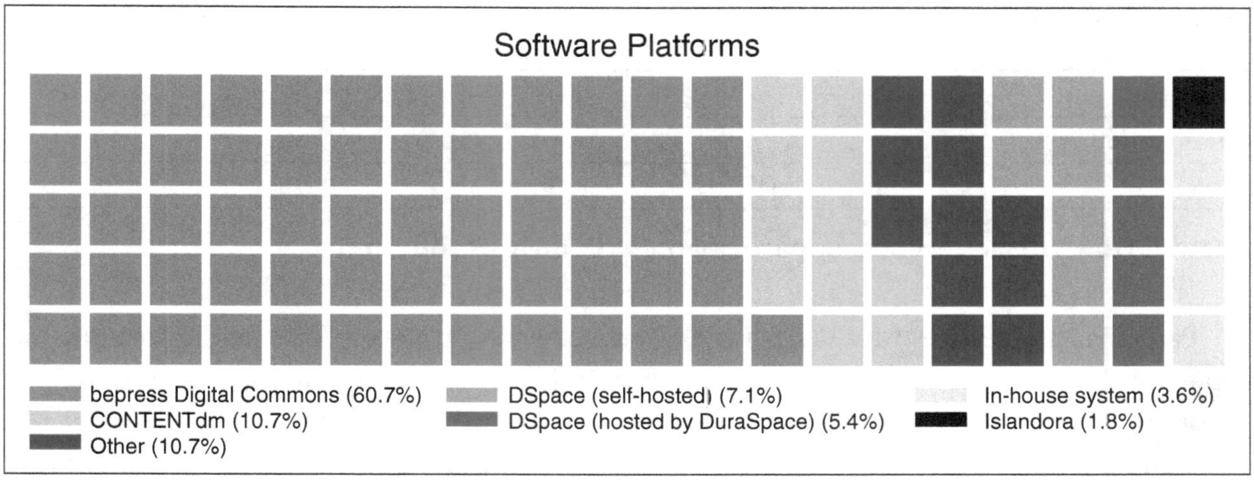

Figure 3: Software platforms selected by participating institutions.

Participants who indicated that their library had chosen an open-source software platform were asked how they handled the setup and customization process for the software. Seven participants (33.3 percent) whose library chose an open-source software answered that "a library staff member setup and customized the software." Five participants (23.8 percent) answered that the "setup and customization was outsourced to an outside vendor." Two participants (9.5 percent) answered that "an employee from another department associated with the institution (such as IT) setup and customized the software." Another seven participants (33.3 percent) answered "other" and offered written comments describing their institution's specific situation. Some of these described a situation where several employees from various areas contributed to the platform's setup (such as a library employee, an IT employee, and the vendor), while others described setup done at a consortial level.

Participants ranked how satisfied they were with their choice of software platform by choosing from Very Unsatisfied, Unsatisfied, Neutral, Satisfied, or Very Satisfied. Fifty-six participants answered this question, with a substantial majority (42 or 75 percent) saying they were either Satisfied or Very Satisfied with their choice of software platform. Only three participants (5.4 percent) said they were either Unsatisfied or Very Unsatisfied, while 11 (19.6 percent) said they were Neutral. The three participants who expressed dissatisfaction with their choice of repository were all using different software options, while the 42 participants who expressed satisfaction were primarily (71.4 percent%) using bepress Digital Commons. One of the unsatisfied participants noted in a comment that their library had switched software platforms several times since launching the IR. Several of the participants who were satisfied with their choice mentioned that the technical support offered by their vendor was part of their positive experience.

Platform	Very Unsatisfied	Unsatisfied	Neutral	Satisfied	Very Satisfied
bepress Digital Commons	0	1	3	15	15
CONTENTdm	1	0	1	3	1
DSpace (hosted or unhosted)	0	0	4	2	1
Islandora	0	0	0	1	0
In-house/other	0	1	3	4	0
Total	1	2	11	25	17

Table 4: How satisfied are survey participants with their IR software?

Participants were asked to rank six criteria for choosing a software platform for their institutional repository by how important each factor was in their decision. Fifty-six participants answered this question, ranking each of the given factors from one to six, with one being the most important. The top-ranked factor overall was "overall costs associated with the software (initial cost of software, annual subscription fees, hosting fees, etc.)" with an average score of 4.20. "Software hosting provided by vendor" was ranked second overall with an average score of 4.09. "Out-of-the-box capability/features" was ranked third with an average score of 3.84. "Technical support offered by vendor" was fourth with an average score of 3.30. "Ease of use" was fifth with an average score of 3.04. "Customizability/flexibility" was ranked sixth with an average score of 2.54.

Options	1	2	3	4	5	6	Score
Overall costs associated with the software (initial cost of software, annual subscription fees, hosting fees, etc.)	19	10	9	6	5	7	4.20
Software hosting provided by vendor	16	14	7	5	6	8	4.09
Out-of-the-box capability/features	14	4	15	11	6	6	3.84
Technical support offered by vendor	1	14	11	11	13	6	3.30
Ease of use	2	8	10	14	14	8	3.04
Customizability/Flexibility	4	6	4	9	12	21	2.54

Table 5: How institutions ranked factors associated with selecting an IR software platform.

The survey asked participants to disclose the primary source of funding for their institutional repository. Fifty-six participants answered this question with the majority (42 participants or 75 percent) saying that the library operating budget was the repository's main source of funding. Nine participants (16.1 percent) said funding came from a combination of sources, and one participant (1.8 percent) said funding was from a special initiative. Four participants (7.1 percent) chose "other" and wrote in that funding was collaborative amongst partners, or came from IT.

Thirty-one participants provided a hard figure for the average cost per year of maintaining the IR (including vendor fees and staffing costs), though many of these figures were approximations, ranges, or the participant offered information about the difficulty of calculating these costs. To analyze the results, any ranges given were rounded up to the highest end of the range. Cost estimates ranged from $3,000 to $100,000 per year with both a median and mode of $18,000 and a mean of $23,413. The table below breaks down the estimated cost by software platform. There are likely to be a large number of possible factors influencing the wide range of total costs estimated by participants, in addition to the platform itself, including services and support provided by the vendor, the amount of storage/server space needed, digitizing costs, and staffing costs.

Software Platform	Count	Lowest Estimated Cost	Highest Estimated Cost	Median Cost
bepress Digital Commons	20	$10,000	$100,000	$21,000
Islandora	1	$15,000	$15,000	$15,000
Other/in-house	6	$3,000	$35,000	$5,500
CONTENTdm	2	$4,000	$7,000	$5,500
DSpace (hosted by DuraSpace)	2	$3,500	$7,000	$5,250

Table 6: Estimated costs of software platforms

Of the "other" software platforms cited in this question, three were DSpace (two were DSpace hosted by Longsight, one was DSpace hosted by a consortium), two were in-house systems, and one was Sobek.

Staffing and Personnel

The section of the survey on staffing and personnel asked participants to answer questions about the employees and departments whose work involves some aspect of managing or maintaining the institutional repository.

Participants were asked who has or had the lead role in planning and implementing the institutional repository. Fifty-six participants answered this question with most (21 participants or 37.5 percent) answering that an unspecified librarian or library staff member had the lead role in planning and implementing the IR. Twelve participants (21.4 percent) answered that it was specifically an institutional repository librarian or scholarly communications librarian (or officer) who took the lead in the repository's implementation. Seven participants (12.5 percent) named the library director in the lead role, while four participants (7.1 percent) named the assistant library director. Another 12 participants (21.4 percent) answered "other," with some of these writing in that an archivist was primarily responsible, or that it was a joint effort between two or more people, or by committee.

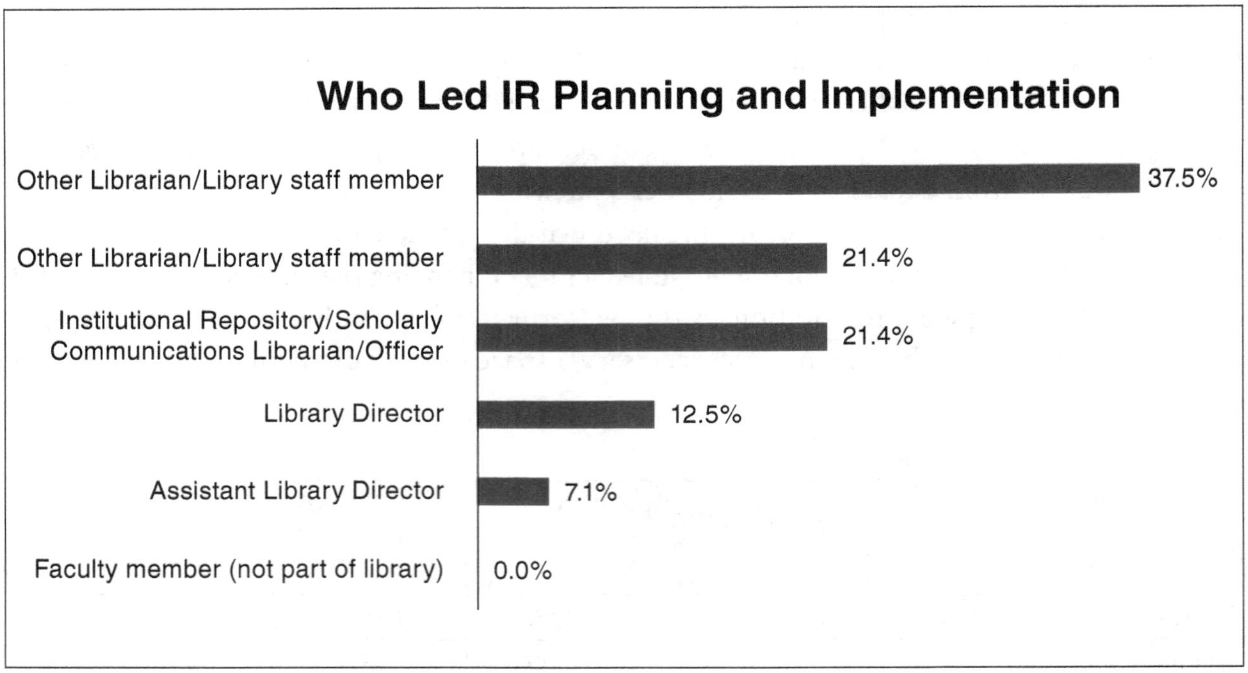

Figure 4: Who had the lead role in implementing the IR?

When asked what department within the institution was primarily responsible for the IR's management, the answers given by 56 participants were much more consistent. Fifty-one participants (91.1 percent) named the library as the department with primary responsibility for the IR. Two participants (3.6 percent) said a consortium was responsible for managing the IR while one participant (1.8 percent) said it was another (non-library) department within the institution. Two participants (3.6 percent) answered "other" and provided the archives and a digital collections center as the departments responsible.

Answers to the question about how the institutional repository is staffed were much more varied. Six options were provided for this question, as well as the option to choose "other" and write in a more specific answer. The only answer choice not selected by any of the 56 respondents was the option that had multiple staff members dedicating 100 percent of their time to managing the IR together. The option selected most frequently was "other," chosen by 18 participants (32.1 percent).

The responses to this question point to the high amount of variation in the way different libraries choose to manage their IRs. Of those who chose "other" and wrote in specific alternatives, seven wrote that one person managed the IR but only devoted a percentage of their time to it. Four wrote that multiple staff contributed part of their time to the IR (with no further explanation of how this differs from the given option below). Three wrote that one person devoted a percentage of their time to managing the IR with help from one student or staff person. One wrote that two librarians devoted a percentage of their time to managing the IR with support from a staff member who devoted 100 percent of their time to the IR. Another wrote that one person devoted 100 percent of their time to the IR with help from one assistant. One wrote that locally one person manages deposits to the IR while at the consortial level there is devoted staff. Finally, one wrote that a single staff person set up the IR but that no one currently actively works on it.

From the given options, fifteen participants (26.8 percent) selected that multiple staff members from other library service areas (not a department dedicated to managing the IR) devote a percentage of their time to managing the IR together. Twelve participants (21.4 percent) selected that one staff member from another library service area devotes a percentage of their time to managing the IR alone. Five participants (8.9 percent) selected that one staff member dedicates 100 percent of their time to managing the IR but has assistance from other staff members who devote a percentage of their time to the IR. Four participants (7.1 percent) selected that one staff member dedicates 100 percent of their time to managing the IR but has assistance from volunteers, student workers, or interns. Two participants (3.6 percent) selected that one staff member dedicates 100 percent of their time to managing the IR alone.

Option	Count	Percent
Other	18	32.1%
Multiple staff members from other library service areas devote a percentage of their time to managing the IR together	15	26.8%
One staff member from another library service area devotes a percentage of their time to managing the IR alone	12	21.4%
One staff member dedicates 100% of their time to managing the IR but has assistance from other staff members who devote a percentage of their time to the IR	5	8.9%
One staff member dedicates 100% of their time to managing the IR but has assistance from volunteers, student workers, or interns	4	7.1%
One staff member dedicates 100% of their time managing the IR alone	2	3.6%
Multiple staff members dedicate 100% of their time to managing the IR together	0	0%

Table 7: Methods for staffing the IR.

The answers to this and other questions from this section suggest that many libraries at small and midsized institutions that have an IR don't necessarily have a Scholarly Communications or other specific department dedicated to its management. The survey asked what other library service areas contribute staff to managing the IR and participants were allowed to choose multiple options as applicable. Fifty-six participants answered this question with most (25 participants or 44.6 percent) answering that Reference/Instruction contributed staff to the IR's management. Sixteen participants (28.6 percent) answered that Cataloging/Acquisitions contributed staff. Fifteen participants (26.8 percent) answered that IT/Technology Services contributed staff. Twelve participants (21.4 percent) answered that no other departments contributed staff to the IR's management, and three participants (5.4 percent) answered that Circulation/ILL contributed staff. Eighteen participants (32.1 percent) answered "other" with eight of these writing in that Archives plays a role in helping to manage the IR. Other areas cited by these participants included Systems, Digital Services, and Special Collections.

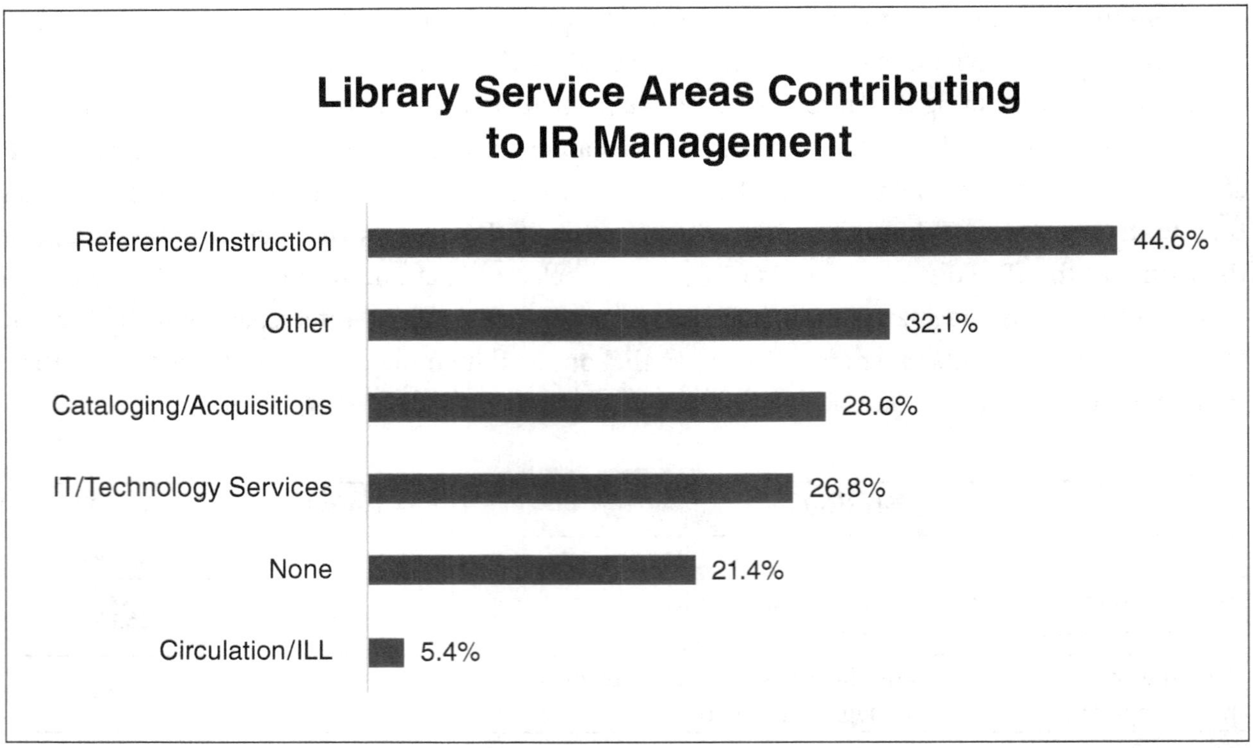

Figure 5: What library services areas contribute to staffing the IR?

Eighteen respondents reported that their IR was staffed by a combination of the four main departments given as options above. The most popular combination of departments was Reference/Instruction and Cataloging/Acquisitions, with five respondents selecting this combination. Four respondents selected a combination of Reference/Instruction, Cataloging/Acquisitions, and Circulation/ILL, and another four respondents selected a combination of Reference/Instruction and IT/Technology Services. Two respondents selected a combination of Cataloging/Acquisitions and IT/Technology Services. One respondent each selected a combination of Reference/Instruction, Cataloging/Acquisitions, and Circulation/ILL; Cataloging/Acquisitions, IT/Technology Services, and Circulation/ILL; and Cataloging/Acquisitions and Circulation/ILL.

Department Combinations	IRs Staff by Combination
Reference/Instruction Cataloging/Acquisitions	5
Reference/Instruction Cataloging/Acquisitions IT/Technology Services	4
Reference/Instruction IT/Technology Services	4
Cataloging/Acquisitions IT/Technology Services	2

Department Combinations	IRs Staff by Combination
Reference/Instruction Cataloging/Acquisitions Circulation/ILL	1
Cataloging/Acquisitions IT/Technology Services Circulation/ILL	1
Cataloging/Acquisitions Circulation/ILL	1

Table 8: Department combinations for staffing the IR.

Policy Development

The section of the survey on policy development asks participants to answer questions regarding policies for the IR, including who can or must submit work to the IR, types and formats of works collected, metadata, and restricting access to content.

The survey asks participants who is authorized to submit content to the IR. Fifty-five participants answered this question and were allowed to choose as many options as were applicable. Fifty participants (90.9 percent) selected that IR staff would upload submissions on behalf of students. Forty-two participants (75.4 percent) selected that IR staff would upload submissions on behalf of faculty. Twenty-four participants (43.6 percent) selected that faculty could upload their own work to the repository. Fifteen participants (27.3 percent) selected that students could upload their own work to the repository. Eight participants (14.6 percent) selected "other" and submitted written answers that included archivists, university staff, or that no one has the option to upload content.

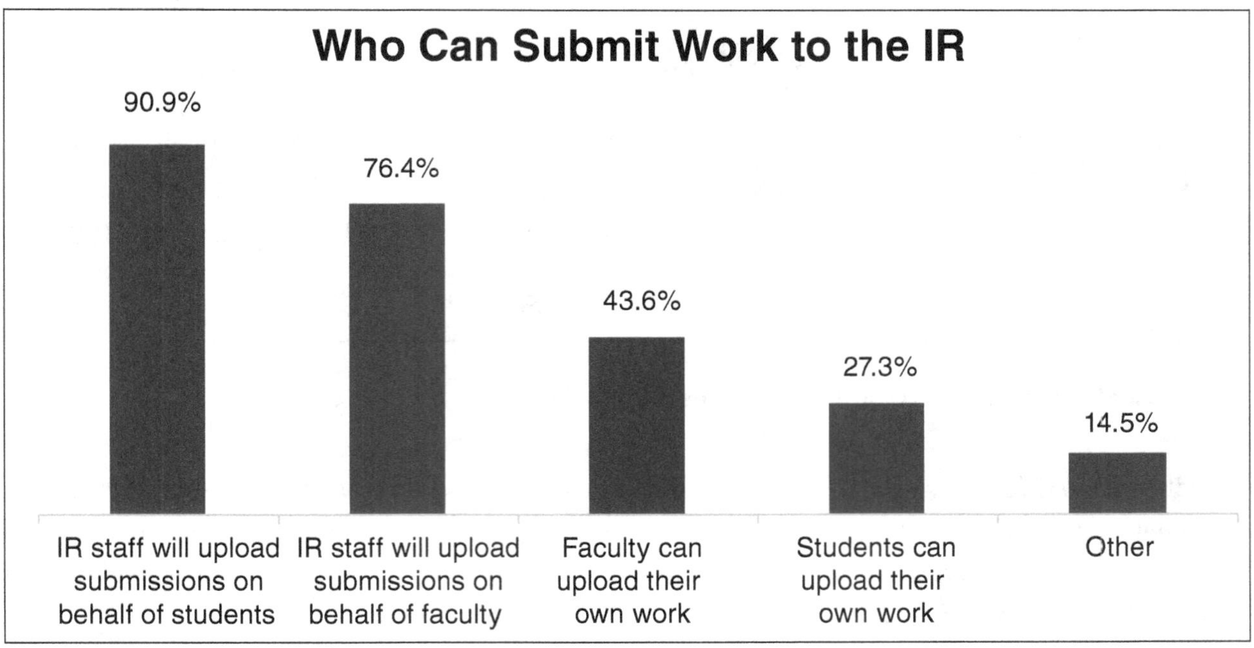

Figure 6: Who can submit work to the IR?

Participants answered in the majority (52 participants or 94.6 percent) that faculty authors at their institutions are not required to deposit their research in the IR by an institutional mandate. Only three participants (5.5 percent) answered that faculty were required to deposit research. The requirements for graduate students were split much more evenly, with 20 participants (36.4 percent) answering that graduate students are required to deposit a digital copy of their thesis or dissertation. Seventeen participants (30.9 percent) answered that graduate students are not required to submit a copy of their thesis or dissertations, while 18 participants (32.7 percent) selected N/A and likely represent undergraduate-only institutions. The majority of participants (42 or 76.4 percent) answered that undergraduate students were not required to deposit a digital copy of any honors papers or capstone projects. Twelve participants (21.8 percent) answered that undergraduate students were required to deposit honors papers or capstone projects, and one participant (1.8 percent) answered with N/A.

The majority of participants (40 or 72.7 percent) do require authors to sign an author release form to deposit their work, while six participants (10.9 percent) answered that they do not. Nine participants (16.4 percent) selected "other." All of these questions were answered by 55 participants each.

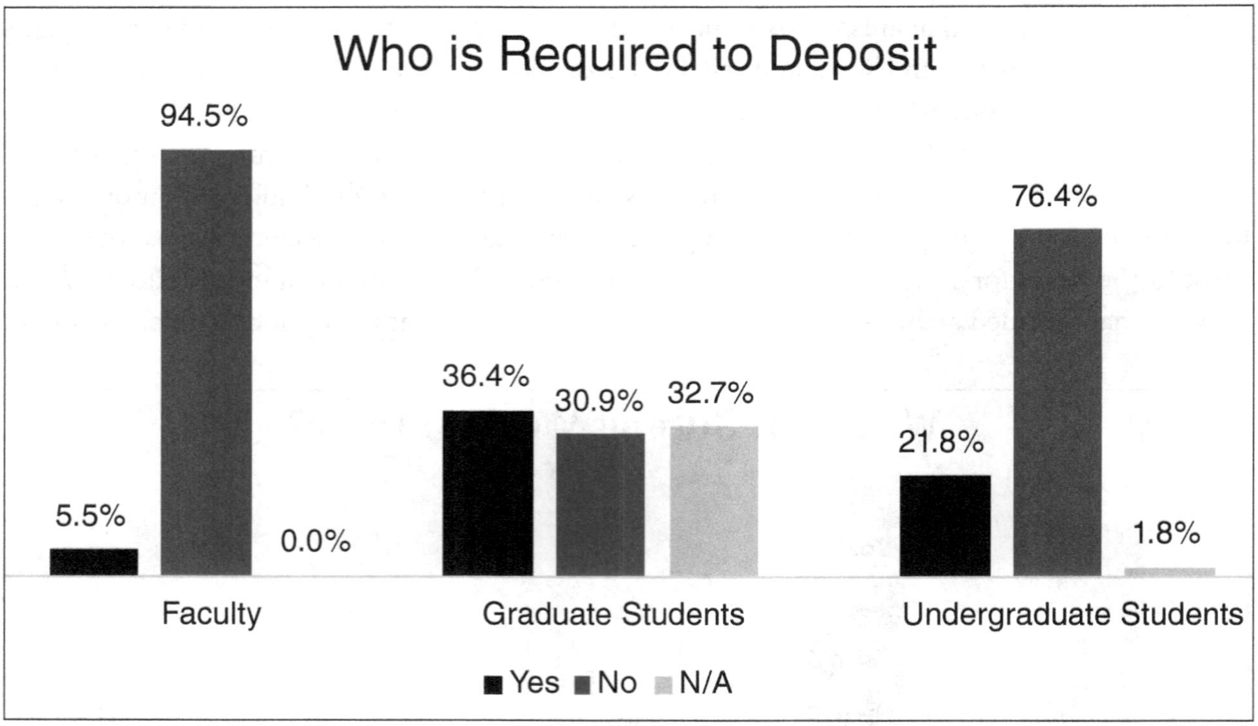

Figure 7: Who is required to deposit work in the IR?

Fifty-five participants also answered the questions regarding what types of content they collect and what formats of content are accepted for submission to the IR. Participants had multiple options to choose from for each question and were allowed to select as many options as applied to their repository. The summary results of both questions are displayed in the tables below:

Type of Content Collected	Count	Percent
Journal articles (preprints, post-prints, etc.)	44	80.0%
Undergraduate honors papers	39	70.9%
Theses and dissertations	38	69.1%
Archival materials	35	63.6%
Conference papers	34	61.8%
Multimedia materials (video, audio, html files)	34	61.8%
Images	33	60.0%
Presentations (slide decks, posters, etc.)	32	58.2%
Student/Faculty journals published by the university	32	58.2%
Book chapters	30	54.5%
Books	30	54.5%
Newsletters	27	49.1%
Reports/Working papers	27	49.1%
Creative works	23	41.8%
Data sets	13	23.6%
Courseware (including syllabi)	7	12.7%
Maps	7	12.7%
Other	7	12.7%

Table 9: Types of content collected.

Formats Collected	Count	Percent
PDF	54	98.2%
JPG	44	80.0%
DOC	37	67.3%
TIFF	33	60.0%
MP4	32	58.2%
PPT	31	56.4%
MP3	30	54.5%
PNG	26	47.3%
WAV	24	43.6%
MPEG	23	41.8%
XLS	21	38.2%
WMV	18	32.7%
PUB	10	18.2%
Other	6	10.9%

Table 10: Formats of content collected.

Participants were also asked if only "born-digital" documents were deposited into the IR, or if non-digital documents were digitized for deposit. Fifty-five participants answered this question and the majority (51 or 92.7 percent) responded that both born-digital and digitized documents are deposited into the IR. Three participants (5.5 percent) answered that only born-digital documents are deposited, while one (1.8 percent) answered that only digitized documents are deposited.

Next, participants were asked how metadata is submitted to the IR, with 55 participants answering this question. Just over half (28 or 50.9 percent) said that metadata is created by a librarian or IR staff member. Eighteen participants (32.7 percent) said that metadata is submitted by the author but reviewed by a librarian or staff member before being uploaded to the IR. Two participants (3.6 percent) said that metadata is submitted by the author and automatically uploaded with their document. Seven participants (12.7 percent) selected "other" with most of the written answers stating that they use some combination of the options provided. Out of the 55 participants who answered, 33 (60 percent) also stated that their library has a policy on minimum requirements for metadata submitted to the IR, while 22 participants (40 percent) said they do not.

Participants were asked what metadata schemes and controlled vocabularies are applied to content in the IR, if any. Fifty-five participants answered these questions and were allowed to select as many options as were applicable from multiple options. The results of those two questions are displayed in the tables below:

Metadata Schemes Used	Count	Percent
Dublin Core	42	76.4%
Custom Scheme	13	23.6%
EAD	6	10.9%
MARC	4	7.3%
Other	4	7.3%
METS	3	5.5%
MODS	2	3.6%
TEI	1	1.8%
PREMIS	0	0.0%

Table 11: Metadata schemes used in the IR.

Controlled Vocabularies Used	Count	Percent
Library of Congress Subject Headings	30	54.5%
Other	25	45.5%
Library of Congress Name Authority File	13	23.6%
Art and Architecture Thesaurus	5	9.1%
Library of Congress Thesaurus for Graphical Materials	5	9.1%
Getty Thesaurus of Geographic Names	3	5.5%
Getty Union List of Artist Names	1	1.8%

Table 12: Controlled vocabularies used in the IR.

A relatively large percentage of participants who answered the question about controlled vocabularies chose "other." Just over half of the responses written in by these participants (52 percent) indicated that they did not use any controlled vocabularies within the system. Five participants (20 percent) said that they use the controlled vocabulary that is built into the repository system, while others indicated that they use local or customized vocabularies. By far the most common metadata scheme was Dublin Core, used in over three-fourths of participants' repositories. Another popular option was using a custom scheme (23.6 percent).

Answers were relatively evenly split on whether or not institutions required user authentication to restrict access to any materials in the IR. Fifty-five participants answered this question and 32 (58.2 percent) said that at least some content was restricted. Twenty-three participants (41.8 percent) answered said they did not restrict content. Participants were also given the opportunity to write in what type of content is restricted in their institution's repository, and all 32 participants who answered that at least some content was restricted provided examples. The most popular type of content to restrict access to was student theses and dissertations, with eight (25 percent) participants citing this content. Seven (21.9 percent) participants reported that private collections of meeting minutes, agendas, university reports, accreditation documents, or trustee files were restricted, while six (18.8 percent) participants reported that they restricted content by the author's request. Four (12.5 percent) participants reported that they restricted access to embargoed content, and two (6.3 percent) reported that university syllabi were restricted. Two (6.3 percent) participants reported that all works in the repository were restricted by campus login, while one (3.1 percent) participant said that only student work was restricted.

Services and Content Development

The section of the survey on services and content development asked participants to answer questions regarding services offered in conjunction with the institutional repository, content solicitation, and promotion of the repository and its related services.

Participants were asked what services are offered in relation to the IR and were permitted to select as many options as were applicable. Fifty-five participants answered this question. The two most common services offered were having IR staff deposit faculty or student work on the author's behalf and metadata/cataloging services, each selected by 44 (80 percent) participants. Also commonly offered were digitization/scanning services, selected by 39 (70.9 percent) participants, author rights consultations, selected by 33 (60 percent) participants, and copyright clearance assistance/requesting permission from publishers, selected by 27 (49.1 percent) participants. Less common offerings were data management planning, selected by 11 (20 percent) participants, and not offering any services, selected by 3 (5.45 percent) participants. Five (9.1 percent) participants chose "other" and wrote in that they offered personal consultation for self-deposit, creation of DOIs, or data conversion.

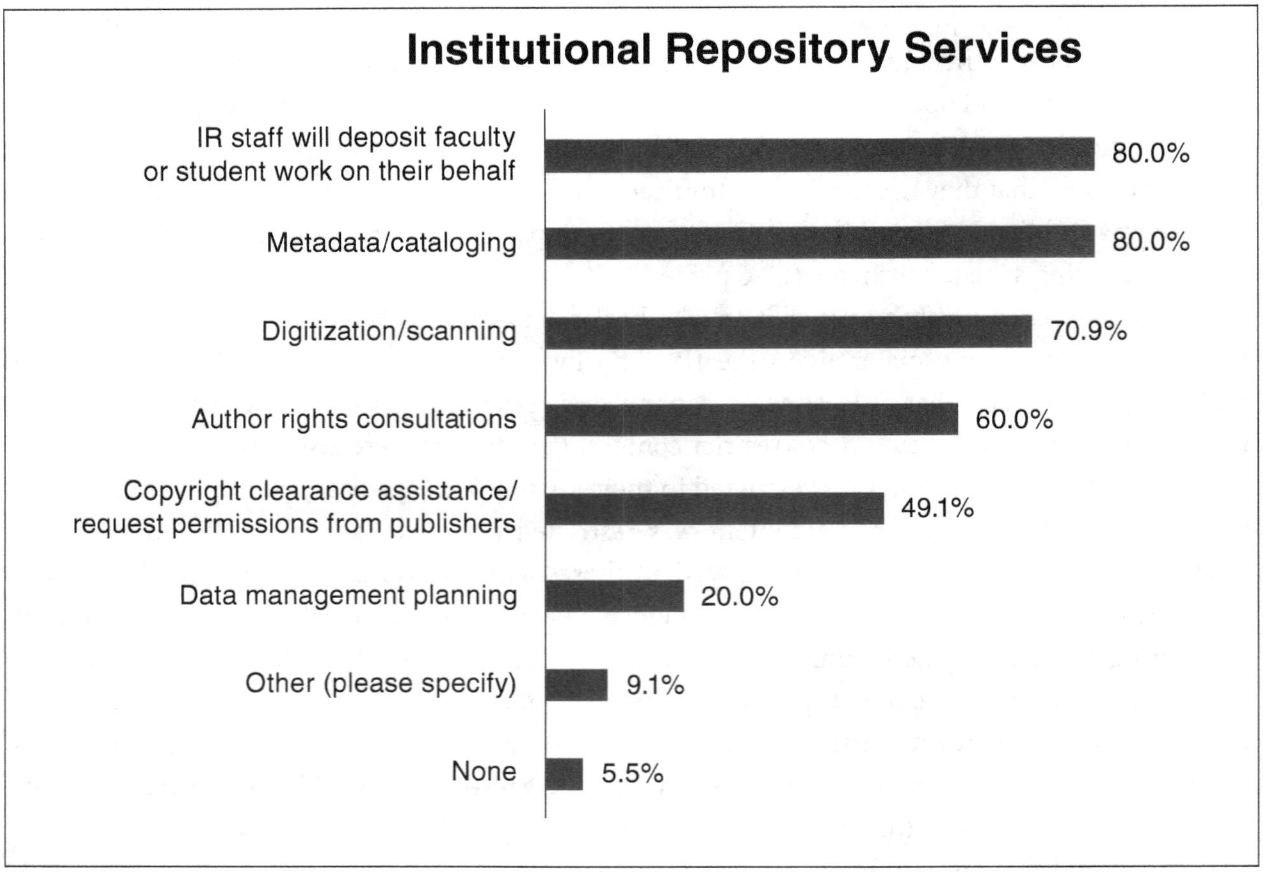

Figure 8: Services offered with the IR.

Asked what methods were used for soliciting content from faculty authors, fifty-five participants answered, selecting as many of the options provided as were applicable. The most common method of solicitation was a regular call for submissions, selected by 25 (45.5 percent) participants, closely followed by having library liaisons reach out to individual faculty and presentations or workshops at faculty department meetings, each selected by 24 (43.6 percent) participants. Other frequently selected methods include requesting CVs from faculty, selected by 20 (36.4 percent) participants, searching databases for faculty publications, selected by 16 (29.1 percent) participants, and none, selected by 15 (27.3 percent) participants. Less common methods of solicitation include offering regular reports to faculty on download statistics, selected by 13 (23.6 percent) participants, and offering individual profile pages for faculty, selected by 9 (16.4 percent) participants. Ten (18.2 percent) participants chose "other." Some examples provided by the participants who chose "other" include that they receive an annual list of faculty publications from the provost's office, that they rely on collaborative pilot projects where department heads or other faculty are approached individually, that they do other specialized presentations and workshops, or that they approach faculty about existing collections that were not previously archived. Others mentioned that they did not have the necessary staff to solicit content from faculty, that they planned to use one or more of these methods but had not yet reached that stage in the process, or that they did not solicit content from faculty because the primary focus of their IR was on other content.

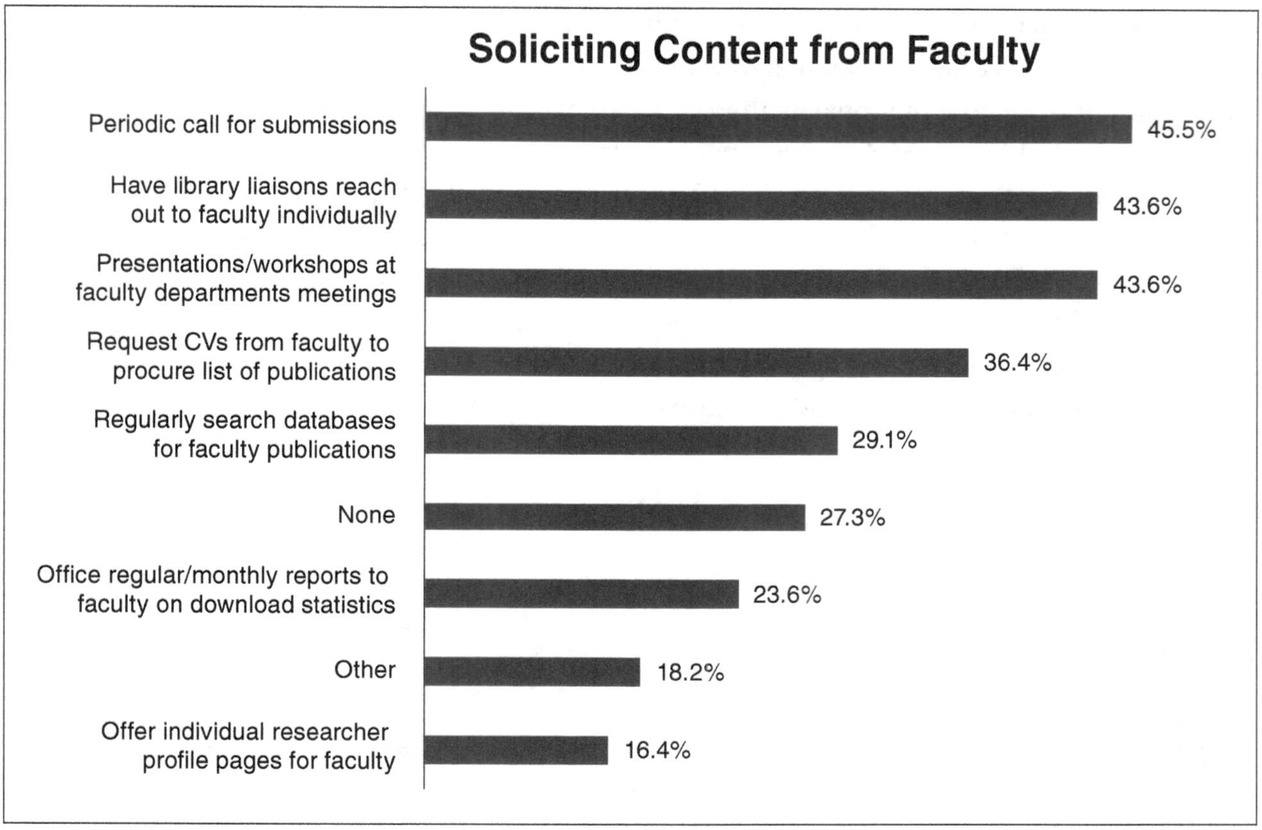

Figure 9: How do institutions solicit content from faculty authors?

Participants were also asked whether or not their IR was prepopulated with a "starter" collection, such as master's theses or a collection of digitized yearbooks, before soliciting content from researchers. Fifty-five participants answered this question, with 30 (54.6 percent) answering in the affirmative and 25 (45.5 percent) answering in the negative. When asked whether any digitization of documents was performed in-house or outsourced, the majority (32 participants or 58.2 percent) said they digitize in-house, while only four (7.3 percent) outsource digitization. However, 17 (30.9 percent) said they do some combination of in-house digitization and outsourcing. Two (3.6 percent) said they do not digitize any documents.

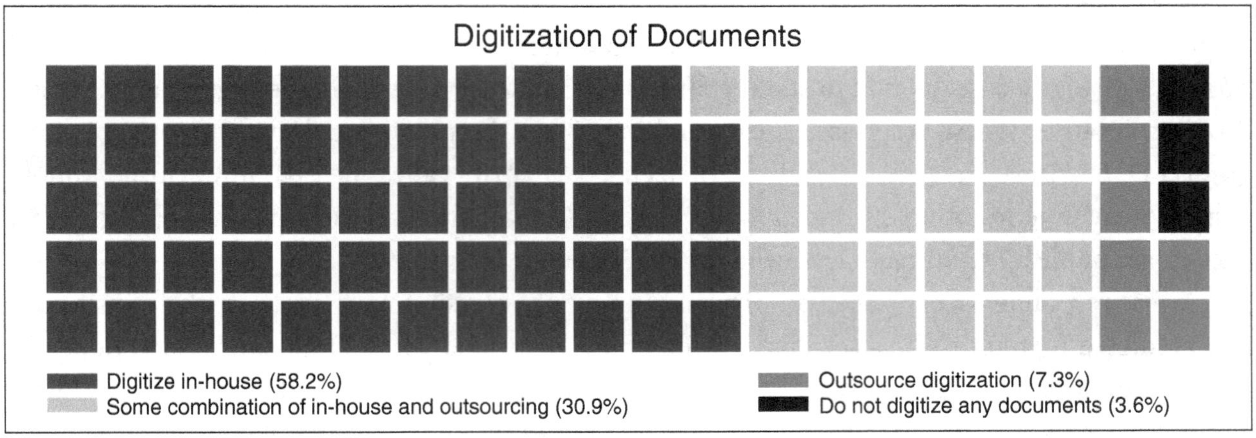

Figure 10: How are documents digitized?

Finally, participants were asked what methods they employ in the IR's promotion. Fifty-five participants answered this question and were permitted to select as many options as applied. The most commonly used promotional method was presentations and workshops at faculty department meetings, selected by 31 (56.4 percent) participants, closely followed by flyers, emails, and other promotional materials, selected by 27 (49.1 percent) participants. Presenting workshops and training about open access, copyright, and other scholarly communication issues, and prominent placement for the IR on the library website were also common, both selected by 25 (45.5 percent) participants. Less common was doing no promotion of the IR, selected by six (10.9 percent) participants. Eight (14.6 percent) participants selected "other," writing in that they met with faculty individually or collaborated with other university departments in the IR's promotion.

Methods of Promotion	Count	Percent
Presentations/workshops at faculty department meetings	31	56.4%
Flyers, emails and other promotional materials	27	49.1%
Prominent placement on library website	25	45.5%
Workshops and training about open access, copyright, and other scholarly communication issues	25	45.5%
Other	8	14.5%
None	6	10.9%

Table 13: How do libraries promote the IR?

All participants, whether their institution had launched an IR or not, were given the chance at the end of the survey to write in any additional comments, and 49 out of 180 participants (27.2 percent) wrote in a response. Of the 49 respondents, 16 (32.7 percent) indicated that they had already started the planning process, had begun the implementation process, or had plans to do so at some point in the future. One participant called it a "high priority" for the year, while another described plans for a consortial repository. Three respondents also discussed the need to pursue funding before the actual implementation could take place, with one currently in the process of writing a CLIR grant to procure funds.

Nearly as many participants (15 or 30.6 percent) wrote about the challenges they face in implementing an IR. The primary challenges mentioned by participants were staffing and overall costs (particularly costs related to staffing and software), with more than one participant calling it "cost-prohibitive;" these responses mirror findings from the professional literature on this topic (Bull & Eden, 2014; Giesecke, 2011; Wu, 2015). One participant called the IR a "low priority" among other library functions they struggled to support, while another mentioned that their faculty "teach more than publish," alluding to less need for an IR at their institution.

A few respondents expressed ambivalence about the possibility of an IR at their institution but predicted it wouldn't be a serious consideration for several years. Others described hopes for further developing IRs that have been created but subsequently neglected. Finally, at least four of the respondents (8.2 percent) described the possibilities of a collaborative partnership, either as their current implementation plan or as the most viable solution for implementing an IR in the future.

The cross-section of responses in the survey results demonstrate that even institutions which all fall into the category of colleges or small universities can display a great disparity in staffing, funding, IT knowledge, and other resources necessary for implementing an institutional repository. However, the repositories created by these institutions show a wide variance in their overall size, construction, and fundamental purpose as well. The results from this survey indicate that there is a broad range of possibility when implementing a repository and that there are a variety of options suited to all sizes and budgets. The sample documentation included below provide examples for institutions in the process of starting their own repositories.

Appendix A. CLIPP Survey with Results

Respondent Information

Q1. Respondent Name

Responses	Count
Open-ended responses	180
Answered question:	**180**
Skipped question:	**0**

Q2. Job Title

Responses	Count
Open-ended responses	180
Answered question:	**180**
Skipped question:	**0**

Q3. Contact Information

Responses	Count
Open-ended responses	180
Answered question:	**180**
Skipped question:	**0**

Institutional information

Q4. Carnegie Classification

Responses	Count
Bac/A&S: Baccalaureate Colleges—Arts & Sciences	47
Bac/Diverse: Baccalaureate Colleges—Diverse Fields	20
Bac/Assoc: Baccalaureate/Associate's Colleges	2
Master's/S: Master's Colleges and Universities (smaller programs)	43
Master's/M: Master's Colleges and Universities (medium programs)	23
Master's/L: Master's Colleges and Universities (larger programs)	19
Answered question:	**154**
Skipped question:	**26**

Q5. Institution Type

Responses	Count
Public	36
Private	118
Answered question:	**154**
Skipped question:	**26**

Q6. FTE Students

Responses	Count
Open-ended responses	154
Answered question:	**154**
Skipped question:	**26**

Q7. FTE Faculty

Responses	Count
Open-ended responses	154
Answered question:	**154**
Skipped question:	**26**

Q8. FTE Librarians

Responses	Count
Open-ended responses	154
Answered question:	**154**
Skipped question:	**26**

Q9. FTE Support Staff

Responses	Count
Open-ended responses	154
Answered question:	**154**
Skipped question:	**26**

Q10. In what stage of planning and implementation is your institution's institutional repository (IR)?

Responses	Count
Have not started any planning for implementing an IR and do not currently have plans to do so	39
Have not started any planning for implementing an IR but have plans to do so at some point in the future	30
Have started planning for implementing an IR but have not yet launched	22
Have launched an IR but no longer actively manage or maintain it (not accepting new deposits, no staff devoted to it)	1
Have launched and currently manage and maintain an IR	57
Answered question:	**149**
Skipped question:	**31**

Q11. When was your IR made available to the public?

Responses	Count
Not yet launched	91
In the last year	6
In the last 2-3 years	14
In the last 4-5 years	19
More than 5 years ago	19
Answered question:	**149**
Skipped question:	**31**

Q12. How many IRs are currently active across your entire institution?

Responses	Count
Zero (0)	86
One (1)	55
Two or more (2+)	8
Answered question:	**149**
Skipped question:	**31**

IR Planning and Implementation

Q13. Did your library/institution conduct a needs assessment prior to implementing the IR?

Responses	Count
Yes	55
No	1
Answered question:	**56**
Skipped question:	**124**

Q14. Do the goals or purpose of your IR directly align with all or part of your institution's mission?

Responses	Count
Yes	55
No	1
Answered question:	**56**
Skipped question:	**124**

Q15. What is the primary purpose of your institution's IR? (primary being the main focus of collection development)

Responses	Count
To collect, preserve, and disseminate faculty research and scholarship	3
To collect, preserve, and disseminate student research and scholarship	6
To collect, preserve, and disseminate all research and scholarship associated with the institution (both student and faculty)	32
To collect, preserve, and disseminate university records and/or archives	7
To collect, preserve, and disseminate teaching and learning materials such as courseware, open-educational resources, and course syllabi	0
To host publications produced by the institution such as student or faculty journals	0
Other (please specify)	8
Answered question:	**56**
Skipped question:	**124**

Q16. What software platform do you use for your IR?

Responses	Count
bepress Digital Commons	34
Eprints	0
DSpace (hosted by DuraSpace)	3
DSpace (self-hosted)	4
Fedora	0
CONTENTdm	6
Islandora	1
Omeka	0
Hydra	0
In-house system	2
Other (please specify)	6
Answered question:	**56**
Skipped question:	**124**

Q17. Rank the following factors by how important they were in deciding on a software platform

Responses	1	2	3	4	5	6	Rating Average
Overall costs associated with the software (initial cost of software, annual subscription fees, hosting fees, etc.)	19	10	9	6	5	7	2.80
Software hosting provided by vendor	16	14	7	5	6	8	2.91
Technical support offered by vendor	1	14	11	11	13	6	3.70
Out-of-the-box capability/features	14	4	15	11	6	6	3.16
Customizability/Flexibility	4	6	4	9	12	21	4.46
Ease of use	2	8	10	14	14	8	3.96
						Answered question:	**56**
						Skipped question:	**124**

Q18. If you chose an open-source software platform, how did you complete the setup and customization process, including any specialized programming work needed to implement the software?

Responses	Count
A library staff member set up and customized the software	7
An employee from another department associated with the institution (such as IT) setup and customized the software	2
Setup and customization was outsourced to an outside vendor	5
N/A	35
Other (please specify)	7
Answered question:	**56**
Skipped question:	**124**

Q19. How satisfied have you been with your choice of software platform?

Responses				Count
Very Unsatisfied	**Unsatisfied**	**Neutral**	**Satisfied**	**Very Satisfied**
1	2	11	25	17
			Answered question:	**56**
			Skipped question:	**124**

Q20. Would you like to make any additional comments about your choice of software platform or other issues related to the implementation of your IR?

Responses	Count
Open-ended responses	26
Answered question:	**26**
Skipped question:	**154**

Q21. What is the main source of funding for the IR?

Responses	Count
Special initiative	1
Grant	0
Library operating budget	42
A combination of funding sources	9
Other (please specify)	4
Answered question:	**56**
Skipped question:	**124**

Q22. What is the average cost per year to maintain the IR (including vendor fees, staffing costs, and any other associated costs)?

Responses	Count
Open-ended responses	37
Answered question:	**37**
Skipped question:	**143**

Staffing and Personnel

Q23. Who has/had the lead role in planning and implementing the IR?

Responses	Count
Library director	7
Assistant library director	4
Institutional Repository/scholarly communications librarian/officer	12
Other librarian/library staff member	21
Faculty member (not part of library)	0
Other (please specify)	12
Answered question:	**56**
Skipped question:	**124**

Q24. What department is primarily responsible for the IR's management?

Responses	Count
Library	51
Non-library institutional department (i.e., Academic Affairs, English department, etc.)	1
Consortium	2
Other (please specify)	2
Answered question:	**56**
Skipped question:	**124**

Q25. How is the IR staffed?

Responses	Count
One staff member dedicates 100% of their time managing the IR alone	2
One staff member dedicates 100% of their time to managing the IR but has assistance from volunteers, student workers, or interns	4
One staff member dedicates 100% of their time to managing the IR but has assistance from other staff members who devote a percentage of their time to the IR	5
Multiple staff members dedicate 100% of their time to managing the IR together	0
Multiple staff members from other library service areas devote a percentage of their time to managing the IR together	15
One staff member from another library service area devotes a percentage of their time to managing the IR alone	12
Other (please specify)	18
Answered question:	**56**
Skipped question:	**124**

Q26. If other library service areas contribute staff to managing the IR, what areas are involved?

Responses	Count
Reference/Instruction	25
Cataloging/Acquisitions	16
IT/Technology Services	15
Circulation/ILL	3
None	12
Other (please specify)	18
Answered question:	**56**
Skipped question:	**124**

Policy Development

Q27. Who is authorized to submit work to the IR? Check all that apply

Responses	Count
Faculty can upload their own work	24
Students can upload their own work	15
IR staff will upload submissions on behalf of faculty	42
IR staff will upload submissions on behalf of students	50
Other (please specify)	8
Answered question:	**55**
Skipped question:	**125**

Q28. Are faculty authors required to deposit their research to the IR by an institutional mandate?

Responses	Count
Yes	3
No	52
Answered question:	**55**
Skipped question:	**125**

Q29. Are graduate students required to deposit a digital copy of their thesis or dissertation?

Responses	Count
Yes	20
No	17
N/A	18
Answered question:	**55**
Skipped question:	**125**

Q30. Are undergraduate students required to deposit a digital copy of any honors papers or capstone projects?

Responses	Count
Yes	12
No	42
N/A	1
Answered question:	**55**
Skipped question:	**125**

Q31. Do you require authors to sign an author release form to deposit their work?

Responses	Count
Yes	40
No	6
Other (please specify)	9
Answered question:	**55**
Skipped question:	**125**

Q32. What type of content do you collect? Check all that apply.

Responses	Count
Courseware (including syllabi)	7
Data sets	13
Books	30
Book chapters	30
Reports/Working papers	27
Conference papers	34
Presentations (slide decks, posters, etc.)	32
Theses and dissertations	38
Undergraduate honors papers	39
Journal articles (preprints, post-prints, etc.)	44
Newsletters	27
Student/Faculty journals published by the university	32
Multimedia materials (video, audio, html files)	34
Images	33
Archival materials	35
Creative works	23
Maps	7
Other (please specify)	7
Answered question:	**55**
Skipped question:	**125**

Q33. What formats do you accept for submissions to the IR? Check all that apply.

Responses	Count
PDF	54
DOC	37
PPT	31
XLS	21
JPG	44
PNG	26
TIFF	33
WAV	24
MP3	30
MP4	32
MPEG	23
WMV	18
PUB	10
Other (please specify)	6
Answered question:	**55**
Skipped question:	**125**

Q34. Do you deposit only "born-digital" documents into the repository, or do you also scan/digitize non-digital documents such as archival images or yearbook collections?

Responses	Count
Only born-digital documents are deposited	3
Both born-digital and digitized documents are deposited	51
Only digitized documents are deposited	1
Answered question:	**55**
Skipped question:	**125**

Q35. How is metadata submitted for IR content?

Responses	Count
Metadata is submitted by the author and automatically uploaded with their file submission	2
Metadata is submitted by the author but reviewed by a librarian/IR staff member before uploading it to the IR	18
Metadata is created by a librarian/IR staff member	28
Other (please specify)	7
Answered question:	**55**
Skipped question:	**125**

Q36. What metadata scheme(s) do you use for materials in the IR? Check all that apply.

Responses	Count
Dublin Core	42
EAD	6
MARC	4
METS	3
MODS	2
PREMIS	0
TEI	1
Custom Scheme	13
Other (please specify)	4
Answered question:	**55**
Skipped question:	**125**

Q37. Do you use any controlled vocabularies? Check all that apply.

Responses	Count
Art and Architecture Thesaurus (AAT)	5
Getty Thesaurus of Geographic Names	3
Getty Union List of Artist Names (ULAN)	1
Library of Congress Name Authority File (LCNAF)	13
Library of Congress Subject Headings (LCSH)	30
Library of Congress Thesaurus for Graphical Materials	5
Other (please specify)	25
Answered question:	**55**
Skipped question:	**125**

Q38. Do you have a policy on minimum requirements for metadata?

Responses	Count
Yes	22
No	33
Answered question:	**55**
Skipped question:	**125**

Q39. Do you protect access to any materials within the IR by requiring user authentication?

Responses	Count
Yes	32
No	23
Answered question:	**55**
Skipped question:	**125**

Q40. If so, what content is protected?

Responses	Count
Open-ended responses	32
Answered question:	**32**
Skipped question:	**148**

Services and Content Development

Q41. What services do you offer in relation to the IR? Check all that apply.

Responses	Count
IR staff will deposit faculty or student work on their behalf	44
Author rights consultations	33
Copyright clearance assistance/request permissions from publishers	27
Digitization/scanning	39
Metadata/cataloging	44
Data management planning	11
None	3
Other (please specify)	5
Answered question:	**55**
Skipped question:	**125**

Q42. What methods do you use to solicit content from faculty? Check all that apply.

Responses	Count
Regular/periodic call for submissions	25
Request CVs from faculty to procure a list of publications	20
Regularly search databases for faculty publications	16
Offer regular/monthly reports to faculty on download statistics	13
Offer individual researcher profile pages for faculty	9
Have library liaisons reach out to faculty individually	24

Responses	Count
Presentations/workshops at faculty department meetings	24
None	15
Other (please specify)	10
Answered question:	**55**
Skipped question:	**125**

Q43. Did you pre-populate the IR with a "starter" collection (i.e., master's theses, digitized yearbook collection, etc.) before soliciting content from researchers?

Responses	Count
Yes	30
No	25
Answered question:	**55**
Skipped question:	**125**

Q44. Do you perform any digitization of documents in-house or outsource digitization work?

Responses	Count
Digitize in-house	32
Outsource digitization	4
Some combination of in-house and outsourcing	17
Do not digitize any documents	2
Answered question:	**55**
Skipped question:	**125**

Q45. What methods do you use to promote the IR? Check all that apply.

Responses	Count
Workshops and training about open access, copyright, and other scholarly communication issues	25
Presentations/workshops at faculty department meetings	31
Prominent placement on library website	25
Flyers, emails and other promotional materials	27
None	6
Other (please specify)	8
Answered question:	**55**
Skipped question:	**125**

Please provide the following information if available:

Q46. Total number of items currently in the IR:

Responses	Count
Open-ended responses	44
Answered question:	**44**
Skipped question:	**136**

Q47. Total number of item views (with or without download):

Responses	Count
Open-ended responses	31
Answered question:	**31**
Skipped question:	**149**

Q48. Total number of item downloads:

Responses	Count
Open-ended responses	37
Answered question:	**37**
Skipped question:	**143**

Q49. Please check below if sample documents can be published in a CLIPP Note publication.

Responses	Count
I give permission to publish any document I send with this completed survey in a CLIPP Note publication.	14
A copyright statement is required to publish any document I send with this completed survey in a CLIPP Note publication.	2
N/A	26
Answered question:	**52**
Skipped question:	**128**

Q50. Please make any additional comments regarding your institution's IR or plans for an IR here:

Responses	Count
Open-ended responses	49
Answered question:	**49**
Skipped question:	**131**

Appendix B. Additional Resources

Center for Research Libraries. (2007). *Trustworthy repositories audit & certification (TRAC): Criteria and checklist.* Retrieved from http://www.crl.edu/sites/default/files/attachments/pages/trac_0.pdf

Confederation of Open Access Repositories. (n.d.). *Resources: Useful reading for repository managers.* Retrieved from https://www.coar-repositories.org/activities/support-and-training/resources.

Crow, R. (2002). *SPARC institutional repository checklist & resource guide.* Retrieved from https://sparcopen.org/wp-content/uploads/2016/01/IR_Guide__Checklist_v1_0.pdf.

Inefuku, H. W. (2013). *Pre-print, post-print or offprint? A guide to publication versions, permissions and the digital repository.* Retrieved from http://lib.dr.iastate.edu/digirep_outreach/2.

Repositories Support Project. (n.d.). *RSP Publications.* Retrieved from http://www.rsp.ac.uk/help/publications/.

Stezano, L. (2016). New ebooklet: *A librarian's process for building an institutional repository.* Retrieved from https://libraryconnect.elsevier.com/sites/default/files/ELS-LC_IR_process.pdf.

Appendix C. Sample Documents

Institution	Sample Documents Provided	Pages
Colgate University Case Library Hamilton, NY	• Submission Policy and Requests for Withdrawal or Updating Content • Guidelines for Preparing Student Works for Submission • Student Work Permission Agreement • Senior Thesis Permission Agreement	p. 55–63
Fairfield University DiMenna-Nyselius Library Fairfield, CT	• Publisher Permission Letter	p. 64
Furman University James B. Duke Library Greenville, SC	• Institutional Repository Guidelines • Submission Process and Agreement • Rights Permission Release	p. 65–73
Grand Valley State University Libraries Allendale, MI	• ScholarWorks Submission Agreement	p. 74–75
Illinois Wesleyan University Ames Library Bloomington, IL	• Non-Exclusive License Agreement—Student	p. 76–78
Lawrence University Seeley G. Mudd Library Appleton, WI	• Policies for Lux	p. 79–83
Pacific University Libraries Forest Grove, OR	• Collection Management Policy • Copyright Policies	p. 84–108
Touro College and University System Libraries New York, NY	• Institutional Repository Policies and Procedures	p. 109–114
University of Nebraska-Lincoln Libraries Lincoln, NE	• Publisher Permission Letter	p. 115
University of South Florida USF Tampa Library Tampa, FL	• Professor Permission Letter	p. 116
Valparaiso University Christopher Center Library Services Valparaiso, IN	• Content Submission Policies and Guidelines • ValpoScholar Services	p. 118–121

Colgate University

Submission Policy and Requests for Withdrawal or Updating Content

Introduction

This document outlines the policies established for the current and future collections residing in Digital Commons @ Colgate.

Submission Policy / Adding Content

Digital Commons @ Colgate is a dynamic institutional repository system, based on the principle of Open Access, that enables us to collect, distribute to the broader community, and preserve the scholarly output of the faculty, students, staff, and their collaborators at Colgate University. Members of the Colgate community interested in submitting materials should consult with the Digital Commons Coordinator. Appropriate content may be added in accordance with the guidelines below:

- The work must be original, produced and submitted (or sponsored by) a faculty, staff, student, organization, or department of Colgate University during the time of their affiliation with the university.
- The work must be creative, scholarly in nature, research-oriented, or of institutional significance.
- The author must own the copyright to all components and content within the work or have received and be able to show permission to have the material available in Digital Commons @ Colgate. The Digital Commons Coordinator will not make a fair use determination of submitted work; such a determination is considered to be the responsibility of the creators.
- The author or representative of the organization or department must sign a permission form prior to material being uploaded to the repository, granting the university the right to distribute and preserve the material via Digital Commons @ Colgate.
- Contributors may include non-affiliated scholars if they are co-authoring with Colgate authors or if they are affiliated closely with the university (e.g., if they are faculty emeriti or hold honorary appointments). Colgate authors should notify all co-authors of intent to deposit work in Digital Commons @ Colgate.

- There is no formal limit to the size of material.
- Various file formats are accepted. Primary documents are converted automatically to the PDF format. Supplementary files can be uploaded in their native format.

Withdrawal of Content

Digital Commons @ Colgate has been established as a permanent repository. Once deposited, an item will not be withdrawn, although under some circumstances it will be removed from view.

- Authors or affected parties may request that works be removed from Digital Commons @ Colgate for reasons of factual inaccuracy, plagiarism, or potential copyright infringement.
- Any requests for withdrawal must be sent to the Digital Commons Coordinator. Requests must state the reason for the withdrawal request and, in the case of potential copyright infringement, must include the following:
    - a physical or electronic signature of the owner, or authorized agent of the owner, of an exclusive right that has allegedly been infringed;
    - clear identification of the copyrighted work(s) claimed to have been infringed;
    - clear identification of the material in Digital Commons @ Colgate that is claimed to be infringing, including the URL(s);
    - reasonably sufficient contact information to allow the Colgate Libraries to contact the complaining party (a mailing address, telephone number, and, if available, an active email address);
    - a statement that the complaining party has a good faith belief that use of the material in the manner complained of is not authorized by the copyright owner, its agent, or the law; and
    - a statement that the information in the notification is accurate and, if applicable, that the complaining party is authorized to act on behalf of the owner of an exclusive right that is allegedly infringed.
- No materials will be removed without an attempt to reach the author of the Digital Commons @ Colgate submission.
- The Colgate University Libraries will respond to all questions or requests for withdrawal within a reasonable amount of time. If the libraries are not able to determine if the use of the work in question is lawful, access to the work through Digital Commons @ Colgate will be removed.
- If authors who have submitted work to Digital Commons @ Colgate leave the university, their work will be retained in the archive. If the authors would like to have new contact information added to their material in Digital Commons @ Colgate, the Digital Commons Coordinator will assist them in having such information added.
- If a work is withdrawn, a citation including original metadata will always remain, but the work is noted as withdrawn.

Updating a Work

The repository is intended to be a permanent scholarly record. Authors may post updated documents. Posting updated versions along with the original material is the preferred way to show the progress of research.

This document originally was prepared by library staff at Linfield College, April 23, 2010, and has been adapted, with the permission of Linfield College, by the Colgate University Digital Commons Steering Committee.

Draft prepared by the Digital Commons Steering Committee, September 17, 2012. Approved by the Digital Services Affinity Group, November 1, 2012.

The Digital Commons Steering Committee reserves the right to change these policies.

~Colgate University Libraries~

Colgate University

Guidelines for Preparing Student Works for Submission to Digital Commons @ Colgate

Student works chosen for the site, with the exception of selected projects with ongoing research, will be accessible on a permanent basis to anyone and fully searchable via Google and Google Scholar.

Digital Commons @ Colgate, an open access initiative (OAI), is just one example of changes that are affecting how scholarship is published and accessed. Digital Commons @ Colgate increases the visibility of our scholarship, but with this increased access comes increased responsibilities.

One significant responsibility is ensuring that your work does not violate the copyrights of others. Copyright protects both you as the author as well as other authors cited by you. Keep in mind that simple keyword searches in Google can reveal when someone has used another's work without giving credit to the original author.

It is also very important when preparing bibliographies or lists of references for your work to pay particular attention to proper citation procedures. You may wish to consult with your faculty mentor or advisor regarding formatting guidelines and styles of documentation. You may also use our subject guide on Citation Style Guides (http://libguides.colgate.edu/CitationStyleGuides) for citation styles. It is in your best interest to become familiar with practices of proper citation in order to avoid charges of plagiarism or copyright infringement. All works submitted to Digital Commons @ Colgate must comply with the Colgate University Academic Honor Code (https://www.colgate.edu/docs/default-source/default-document-library/honor-code8-20.pdf?sfvrsn=2).

If your research involves human subjects, it must follow the guidelines and procedures of Colgate's Institutional Review Board (see http://www.colgate.edu/academics/departments-and-programs/psychology/institutional-review-board).

If you have questions about these guidelines, please contact the Digital Commons Coordinator (digitalcommons@colgate.edu).

This document originally was prepared by library staff at Linfield College and has been adapted, with the permission of Linfield College, by the Colgate University Digital Commons Steering Committee.

Draft prepared by the Digital Commons Steering Committee, October 18, 2012. Approved by the Digital Services Affinity Group, November 1, 2012.

The Digital Commons Steering Committee reserves the right to change these policies.

Colgate University

Student Work Permission Agreement

By signing the form below, I grant Colgate University the non-exclusive perpetual right to distribute my submission ("the Work") over the internet and/or make it part of the university's digital archive for scholarship (if applicable), currently Digital Commons @ Colgate, or its successor technology. I further grant to Colgate University the right to transfer the Work to any format or medium now known or later developed for preservation and access in accordance with this agreement. Nothing in this agreement with Colgate University affects or changes the work's copyright status. Only materials made part of the university's digital archive will be preserved in perpetuity in order to sustain the scholarly record.

I warrant that:

1. The Work is my original work and does not, to the best of my knowledge, infringe or violate any rights of others nor does the deposit violate any applicable laws.
2. I have the authority and/or have obtained all necessary rights to permit Colgate University to use, duplicate, and distribute the Work and that any third-party owned content is clearly identified and acknowledged within the Work.
3. I release the university from any liability whatsoever in connection with its use of the Coursework (and my name).
4. I hereby authorize and consent to the release, maintenance, and display of my name, status as a student at Colgate, and any other personal information I have provided in connection with the Work itself and any associated information.

The Contributor specifically acknowledges that the Content may constitute an educational record under FERPA (20 U.S.C. § 1232g) and expressly consents to the use of the Content as contemplated under this Agreement.

By granting this non-exclusive license, I acknowledge that I have read and agreed to the terms of this agreement and all related Colgate University policies.

Contributor Information:

Signature ____

Name (please print): ______________________ Date: ______________

Email: ____

Identification of Content

Title of content: ____

Author(s): ____

Semester content was created: ____

Course name/number: ____

Associated faculty: ____

Content type: ____

Adapted from the Illinois Wesleyan University Non-Exclusive License Agreement and NYU Permission to Use Student Work form.

Drafted 091313. Updated 013114 DAK, SK, SK. Approved by JAS, KL 02032014.

Colgate University

Senior Thesis Permission Agreement

By signing the form below, I grant Colgate University the non-exclusive perpetual right to make available my submission ("the Work") over the internet and/or make it part of the university's digital archive for scholarship (if applicable), currently Digital Commons @ Colgate, or its successor technology. I further grant to Colgate University the right to transfer the Work to any format or medium now known or later developed for preservation and access in accordance with this agreement. Nothing in this agreement with Colgate University affects or changes the Work's copyright status (see university policy on intellectual property for further information). Only materials made part of the university's digital archive will be preserved in perpetuity in order to sustain the scholarly record.

I warrant that:

1. The Work is my original work and does not, to the best of my knowledge, infringe or violate any rights of others nor does the deposit violate any applicable laws.
2. I have the authority and/or have obtained all necessary rights to permit Colgate University to use, duplicate and distribute the Work and that any third-party owned content is clearly identified and acknowledged within the Work.
3. I release the university from any liability whatsoever in connection with its use of the Work (and my name).
4. I hereby authorize and consent to the release, maintenance and display of my name, status as a student at Colgate, and any other personal information I have provided in connection with the Work itself and any associated information.

I specifically acknowledge that the Work may constitute an educational record under FERPA (20 U.S.C. § 1232g) and expressly consent to the use of the Work as described under this Agreement (see the Registrar's policy on FERPA for further information).

By granting this non-exclusive license, I acknowledge that I have read and agreed to the terms of this agreement and all related Colgate University policies.

Author Information:

Signature ____

Name (please print): ______________________ Date: ________________

Email: ______________________ Graduating class year: ________________

Identification of Thesis (please print)

Title of thesis: ____

Department: ____

Primary faculty advisor: ____

Additional faculty advisors: ____

____

Is there additional content associated with the thesis? (video, image, or data files, separate appendices, etc.) ❑ Yes ❑ No

If yes, list file names of additional content, or the URL for a streaming file:

Choose the statement below that defines how you want to share your thesis. The first statement provides the most access to your work; the last statement provides the least access.

- ❒ I agree to make all content available to Colgate University community *and* to the larger scholarly community upon its deposit in our permanent digital archive, Digital Commons @ Colgate, or its successor technology.
- ❒ I agree to make all content available to the Colgate University community only upon its deposit in our permanent digital archive, Digital Commons @ Colgate, or its successor technology.
- ❒ I agree to submit all content for deposit in the permanent digital archive, Digital Commons @ Colgate, or its successor technology, but the content cannot be made available. (A metadata record for the thesis will be available.)
- ❒ I agree to have the metadata for the thesis in the permanent digital archive, Digital Commons @ Colgate, or its successor technology, but I do not wish to submit any content.
- ❒ I do not want any content or metadata in the permanent digital archive, Digital Commons @ Colgate, or its successor technology.

Temporary Restriction (Embargo)
Embargo options should be discussed with and approved by the faculty advisor(s).

Senior Thesis Advisor Approval (to be completed by the faculty advisor(s))

Honors Designation (check one):
❒ None ❒ Honors ❒ High Honors

Access (check one):
- ❒ I agree with the student's access indication.
- ❒ I disagree with the student's access indication, and the thesis should be further restricted: (check one):
  - ❒ Colgate login access only
  - ❒ Metadata only; no access to content
  - ❒ No metadata or content

Embargo (check one if applicable): ❒ 6 months ❒ 1 year ❒ 2 years ❒ 5 years

____

Signature of Primary Faculty Advisor: Date:

____

Signature of Additional Faculty Advisors: Date:

____

Signature of Additional Faculty Advisors: Date:

---

* Adapted from the Colgate University "Student Work Permission Agreement" and the Linfield College "Student Thesis Submission Form." 12/2015

Fairfield University

Publisher Permission Letter

I am writing on behalf of the DigitalCommons@Fairfield repository (http://digitalcommons.fairfield.edu) and [insert faculty member name here]. The institutional repository is a service of the DiMenna-Nyselius Library at Fairfield University for academic authors, providing open access to the full-text of their publications. All content includes full bibliographic details, a copyright notice, and a link back to the publisher or journal homepage, if requested.

I'm writing to seek your permission to include the final publisher PDF version of this article in our repository:

- [insert citation here]

Kindly contact me (at digitalcommons@fairfield.edu) to give your permission for including the article in DigitalCommons@Fairfield. Please also include any further requirements you may have. In the event that the final PDF version is not permitted, please consider granting permission for us to include the author's post-print.

If you do not solely control copyright in the requested materials, I would appreciate any information you can provide about others to whom I should write, including most recent addresses if available.

Thank you for your consideration of this request. I look forward to your reply.

Sincerely,

Nina Peri
Project Coordinator, DigitalCommons@Fairfield
DiMenna-Nyselius Library
Fairfield University
1073 North Benson Road
Fairfield, Connecticut 06824
digitalcommons@fairfield.edu

*Furman University Scholar Exchange (FUSE)**

Institutional Repository Guidelines

About FUSE

A. Introduction

The Furman University Scholar Exchange (FUSE) is an open access collection of scholarly, research, and creative works produced by faculty, students, staff, and other members of the Furman community. FUSE is administered by the Furman University Libraries in cooperation with individual departments and academic units of the University.

B. Mission

FUSE collects the varied and diverse scholarly and research output of Furman University in one digital space, enabling the University to effectively promote and exchange the ideas produced by Furman scholars.

This collection strives to remove barriers to information access by freely and openly disseminating scholarship produced by Furman University faculty, students, staff, academic/administrative units, and other members of the Furman community. FUSE supports open access (OA) which expands shared knowledge and accelerates multi-disciplinary breakthroughs in research. FUSE records are accessible to the public and fully searchable by online search engines such as Google Scholar. As such, priority is given to works where the full-text is deposited into FUSE for public sharing.

C. Administrative Responsibilities

Furman University Libraries is responsible for administering FUSE. This includes but is not limited to implementation, policies and guidelines, strategies, training, and ongoing assessment.

FUSE administrators are responsible for: determining and maintaining the structure and organization of FUSE, establishing collection and use guidelines for FUSE, educating users about the requirements of copyright law, coordinating with library liaisons on subject-specific projects, and approving/coordinating the creation of new projects, especially those that will require additional staff time, storage space, emerging formats, or digitization.

* Wright, Andrea M. and Allen, Christy, "Furman University Scholar Exchange (FUSE) Institutional Repository Guidelines" (2014). Libraries Institutional Records. 1. https://scholarexchange.furman.edu/lib-records/1/.

Library faculty and staff are responsible for communicating the purpose of FUSE to the Furman University community, recruiting materials for inclusion in FUSE, educating users in the basic use of the system, and referring projects to the FUSE administrators as required.

Current members of the Furman community may submit materials for inclusion in FUSE, and/or work with the FUSE administrators to coordinate the creation of new projects as required.

Department, Program, Institute, Event, or Journal representatives are responsible for ensuring that submissions meet the FUSE guidelines for inclusion, approving/coordinating content to their specific collections, and coordinating with FUSE administrators on the creation of new projects.

Scholars interested in contributing to FUSE may contact their library liaison or the FUSE administrators at scholarexchange@furman.edu.

D. Content Organization

Content within FUSE is organized hierarchically into communities and sub-communities. The individual scholarly works themselves live in collection series, conferences, journals, and image galleries. Each community, sub-community, collection series, conference, journal, image gallery, and specific item has its own individual permanent URL to facilitate sharing and linking to these specific areas within FUSE.

See the table below for more specific information:

High-Level Organization of FUSE

Name	Description	Digital Commons Classification[1]
Departments, Centers, and Institutes	Contains one sub-community for each department, center, institute, and program on campus. Each of these sub-communities will also contain collection series broken down by type of scholarship. Commonly used collection series include "presentations," "publications," and "theses and dissertations."	Community
Academic Events	Contains all the "conferences" hosted in FUSE.	Community
Curriculum Materials	Contains all the "Curriculum Materials" hosted in FUSE.	Collection Series
Journals	Contains all the "journals" hosted in FUSE.	Community
University Records and Archives	Contains collection series for University records and Archives materials: such as "Annual Reports," "Newsletters," "Promotional Materials," etc.	Community
Faculty Scholarship	Mirrors all content in the "Departments, Centers, and Institutes" community where the "Scholarship Type" of a specific item is defined as "Faculty Scholarship."	Collection Series
Student Scholarship	Mirrors all content in the "Departments, Centers, and Institutes" community where the "Scholarship Type" of a specific item is defined as "Student Scholarship."	Collection Series

[1]This column lists the back-end hierarchy structure provided by the platform provider Digital Commons. It is listed here mainly as a reference for the FUSE administrators.

FUSE Content Guidelines

Below you will find guidelines related to appropriate content for FUSE. FUSE Administrators reserve the right to accept or reject any content, in part or in whole, submitted to FUSE, and to remove any content found to be in violation of the Submission Agreement.

A. Who may submit content?

Content may be submitted to FUSE by:

- ❒ Current and retired faculty at Furman University
- ❒ Current students at Furman University
- ❒ Current staff at Furman University

B. What materials may be contributed?

FUSE administrators have established the following collection priorities. This list is not meant to be comprehensive. Other forms of scholarship will be considered for inclusion. Please contact FUSE administrators at scholarexchange@furman.edu if you have any questions or concerns.

- ❒ Published scholarship. Priority will be given to version of record, then post-print, and then pre-print
- ❒ Theses, dissertations, and senior projects/papers
- ❒ Academic presentations and posters
- ❒ Creative works and performances
- ❒ Academic events sponsored by the university, faculty, or staff. Possible examples may include:
    - ✧ Conferences
    - ✧ Lectures
    - ✧ Workshops and professional development
    - ✧ Proceedings
- ❒ Publications produced by Furman faculty, students, and staff. Possible examples may include:
    - ✧ Peer-reviewed publications
    - ✧ Publications hosted online through FUSE
    - ✧ Back files of Furman-produced publications
- ❒ Curriculum materials as deemed appropriate by the FUSE administrators. Possible examples may include:
    - ✧ Labs
    - ✧ Syllabi
    - ✧ Lesson plans
- ❒ Data sets

- ❒ University records as deemed appropriate by the FUSE administrators. Possible examples may include:
    - ✧ Departmental publications
    - ✧ Annual reports
    - ✧ Committee/council meetings minutes
- ❒ Metadata records for research/scholarship that link to an openly accessible, full-text version hosted on another site
- ❒ Metadata records for research/scholarship where the intention is to supply the full text once the publishing embargo has been lifted

C. What file formats are accepted?

FUSE will accept most common file formats. The Administrators retain the right to accept, reject, convert, and optimize file format and size for download and distribution.

D. Who owns the copyright of the deposited content?

Submission Agreement

Prior to submitting content to FUSE, a contributor will be required to accept a Submission Agreement. The Agreement states that the Contributor of the Work must either own the rights to the Work or must have written permission from the rights holder to submit it to FUSE.

If a Contributor accepts the Submission Agreement, they are granting FUSE, on behalf of Furman University, a non-exclusive, royalty-free License to distribute the Work. All other intellectual property rights remain unchanged. If a Contributor owns the rights to the Work, s/he will continue to maintain those rights and the responsibility for enforcing them. Contributors retain the right to revoke the non-exclusive license by contacting scholarexchange@furman.edu.

Co-Authors

If the Work was written by two or more authors, each joint author has the ability to grant a non-exclusive license (by accepting the Submission Agreement) without the permission of other joint author(s). The FUSE policy is as follows:

- Any co-author can give permission for deposit.
- Any co-author can object and request take-down, which will be honored.
- In cases of disagreement, the full text will be suppressed or will be removed until the co-authors can reach an agreement about its status.

To prevent potential disagreements between co-authors, it is recommended that you talk to your co-author(s) prior to submitting to FUSE.

Pre-publication and Publishing Embargoes

In some cases, a publisher or author may request an embargo on distributing a full work through FUSE.

The author may submit a metadata record to FUSE that includes an expected date of FUSE publication in the Comments field and a link to the publisher version of the full work. Once the embargo period has passed, the author should submit the electronic version of the work along with any additional updates to the metadata record to the FUSE administrators at scholarexchange@furman.edu.

Creative Commons Licenses

A Contributor who is also the Rights Holder may choose to make their Work available online under a Creative Commons License. During submission, contributors will have the option of selecting the Creative Commons license that they would like applied to that Work. Selecting a Creative Commons License is optional. Read more about Creative Commons here: http://creativecommons.org/licenses/.

E. What are the guidelines for revising and removing content?

Revising Content

Authors may revise their submissions through their FUSE accounts prior to those submissions being posted online by administrators. Authors can request revisions to their content after the work has been posted to FUSE by contacting either the administrators of the collection(s) to which their work was submitted or by contacting the FUSE administrators at scholarexchange@furman.edu. Please include the reason for revision in this contact.

Removing Content

The full text of a Work may be removed from FUSE by sending a request to the FUSE administrators at scholarexchange@furman.edu. If the Work is removed, a record describing the original version of the paper will always remain on the site at the same URL.

F. What are the rights and terms of use for users of the IR?

- All users must respect the intellectual property rights of the copyright owner.
- For previously published works (journal articles, book chapters, etc.) for which the publisher retains copyright, permission has been granted (where necessary) to post this material in FUSE. For any use which exceeds personal use or fair use under US copyright law, permission may be required by the copyright owner of the material.
- For previously unpublished scholarly or creative works, the right to download or print any portion of this material is granted by the copyright owner only for personal or educational use. The author/creator retains all proprietary rights, including copyright ownership. Any editing, other reproduction or other use of this material by any means requires the express written permission of the copyright owner.

- Material may not be copied, distributed, displayed, altered, or used for commercial purposes unless specified by a Creative Commons License.
- Except as provided above, or for any other use that is allowed by fair use (Title 17, §107 U.S.C.), you may not reproduce, republish, post, transmit, or distribute any material from this website in any physical or digital form without the permission of the copyright owner (not necessarily the author) of the material.

FUSE Scholar Profile Content Guidelines

FUSE Scholar Profiles are created on the platform SelectedWorks. Scholars with existing profiles may affiliate their profile with Furman University which will apply Furman branding and colors. Scholars may also create new profiles and affiliate them with Furman. The scholar will retain their Scholar Profile, all the content in the profile, and the ability to continue to change and update their profile, even if the scholar is no longer affiliated with Furman University. When the scholar leaves the university, they should unaffiliate themselves with Furman. The FUSE Administrators reserve the right to unaffiliate scholars as needed.

A. Who may create a profile?

A Scholar Profile may be created by:

- Current and retired faculty at Furman University
- Current students at Furman University
- Current staff at Furman University

B. What materials may be contributed?

Content which has been submitted to FUSE or other instances of Digital Commons can be automatically imported into Scholar Profiles. By submitting the work to FUSE before adding to a Scholar Profile, readership statistics on the item will remain consolidated. For this reason, it is recommended that work which Furman scholars would like to make openly accessible be submitted first to FUSE and then imported into Scholar Profiles.

Scholars may also include items which are not appropriate for inclusion in FUSE in the Scholar Profile. This could include but is not limited to: links to authored books on third-party websites, links to toll-access journal articles, personal writings, and blogs. Scholars are responsible for obtaining appropriate copyright permissions for any direct posting of work to their Scholar Profile.

Contact Information

Scholars interested in contributing to FUSE may contact their library liaison or the FUSE administrators at scholarexchange@furman.edu.

*Furman University Scholar Exchange (FUSE)**

Submission Process and Agreement

Submission Process

Follow the instructions below to submit to The Furman University Scholar Exchange (FUSE). Before submitting, please read all relevant policies and/or submission guidelines.

The submission process consists of the following steps:

1. Read and accept the Submission Agreement below.
2. Provide information about yourself and any co-authors.
3. Provide information about the Work that you are submitting.
4. Upload your electronic file and associated files.

Before you begin, please be sure you have the following items:

- The submission's title
- An abstract (up to 250 words)
- A list of keywords (10 maximum)
- The electronic format of your file, or hyperlink to your file, if any

Submission Agreement

This Non-Exclusive License Agreement ("Agreement") is hereby made between the Contributor and Furman University.

By checking the box below, I grant The Furman University Scholar Exchange (FUSE) on behalf of Furman University a perpetual, non-exclusive, worldwide, royalty-free License to use, display, distribute, transmit, publish, reproduce, or copy the Work either digitally, in print, or in any other medium. For purposes of this Agreement, Work means the audio, visual, textual, graphical, or other materials provided by the Contributor under this Agreement. Other than the License granted herein, the Contributor retains all intellectual property rights to the Work and the responsibility for enforcing those rights. The Contributor retains the right to revoke the non-exclusive license granted hereunder upon written notice to scholarexchange@furman.edu. Upon receipt of such written notice, the FUSE Administrators will, within ninety (90) days, cease and desist from using the Work on FUSE.

---

* Wright, Andrea M. and Allen, Christy, "Furman University Scholar Exchange (FUSE) Institutional Repository Guidelines" (2014). Libraries Institutional Records. 1. https://scholarexchange.furman.edu/lib-records/1/.

To the best of my knowledge, I warrant as follows:

1. that I have the full power and authority to make this agreement;
2. that I am the sole owner of the Work or that I have secured all necessary licenses, consents, and authorizations with respect to the use of the Work;
3. that no part of the Work violates or infringes upon the patent rights, copyrights, trade secrets, trademarks, or constitutes defamation, invasion of privacy, or the violation of any right of publicity or other rights of any person or entity.

I specifically acknowledge that:

1. if the Work contains any material of which I am not the original author/designer, then I must: (a) provide written permission from the copyright holder of said material as an additional file attached to the submission; or (b) remove the material from the Work;
2. the Work may constitute an educational record under FERPA (20 U.S.C. § 1232g), and I expressly consent to the use of the Work as contemplated under this Agreement.

Furman University reserves the right to accept or reject any content, in part or in whole, submitted to the Furman University Scholar Exchange, and to remove any content found to be in violation of this Submission Agreement.

This Agreement shall be governed by and construed under applicable federal laws and the laws of the State of South Carolina, and the parties expressly agree that jurisdiction and venue of any dispute shall exclusively be in Greenville County, South Carolina.

For further details on Furman University Scholar Exchange's mission, collection policies, and practices, please read the Furman University Scholar Exchange (FUSE) Institutional Repository Guidelines.

Please print this page for your records.

*Furman University Scholar Exchange (Fuse)**

Rights Permission Release

This release grants Furman University a perpetual, non-exclusive, worldwide, royalty-free License to distribute the following material(s) as part of the institutional repository Furman University Scholar Exchange (FUSE) (http://scholarexchange.furman.edu/). Furman University agrees to provide appropriate attribution for the material(s). The rights holder(s) retain all rights and permissions for this work. Any use beyond those described in the FUSE Institutional Repository Guidelines (http://scholarexchange.furman.edu/lib-records/1/) shall require written approval from the rights holder(s).

Permissions for this release were granted by:

PUBLISHER ______________________________

PUBLISHER CONTACT ______________________________

DATE ______________________________

* Wright, Andrea M. and Allen, Christy, "Furman University Scholar Exchange (FUSE) Institutional Repository Guidelines" (2014). Libraries Institutional Records. 1. https://scholarexchange.furman.edu/lib-records/1/.

Grand Valley State University

ScholarWorks Submission Agreement

ScholarWorks@GVSU is an open-access repository maintained by the Grand Valley State University (GVSU) Libraries to showcase, preserve, and provide access to the scholarly and creative work produced by the GVSU community. For more information, email scholarworks@gvsu.edu, or visit our webpage at http://scholarworks.gvsu.edu/about.html.

Type your initials next to ***one*** *of the following options:*

______ I agree to grant the GVSU Libraries a non-exclusive license to provide online **open access** to my submitted scholarly/creative work via ScholarWorks@GVSU. *You retain all copyright in your work, but you give us permission to make it available online for anyone to read and to preserve it in ScholarWorks@GVSU.*

______ I agree to grant the GVSU Libraries a non-exclusive license to provide **limited access** to my scholarly/creative work to the GVSU community via ScholarWorks@GVSU. *You retain all copyright in your work, but give us permission to make it available to users logged in to the GVSU network, and to preserve it in ScholarWorks@GVSU. The public abstract and the title of your work will be visible online for anyone to see, but your full work will only be available to the GVSU community.*

______ I would like to opt out and not have this work available in the repository.

Embargo—Optional: *(You may choose to restrict electronic access to your work for up to three years from the date the work is submitted to ScholarWorks. When the embargo expires, your work will become available. This process is automatic, so if you need to change the embargo period after you have submitted your work, please contact us.*

Note: your title and public abstract will still be visible online during the embargo. *If your title or abstract contains confidential, patent-related, or sensitive information, please ensure you change it.)*

Length of Embargo: ____

Keywords: *(Provide several relevant words that describe the content of your work.)*

____

____

____

Public Abstract/Description: *(Provide a short description of your work. You may use the abstract from your work, modify it, or create a new description. This will be available online even if your work is under an embargo, so you may want to remove any patent-related or sensitive information in the abstract.)*

____

____

____

I warrant as follows:

1. I hold the copyright to this work and agree to permit this work to be posted in the ScholarWorks@GVSU institutional repository.
2. I understand that accepted works may be posted immediately as submitted unless I request otherwise.
3. I have read, understand, and agree to abide by the policies of ScholarWorks@GVSU. (Our policies can be found at: http://scholarworks.gvsu.edu/about.html.)

By typing my name into the Author field, I am agreeing to the terms above and attaching my electronic signature. I understand that if I do not agree to these terms, I should not type my name.

Title: ____

Author: _______________________________ Date:__________________

Faculty Member/Advisor: ____

Date: ____

Illinois Wesleyan University

Non-Exclusive License Agreement—Student

This Non-Exclusive License Agreement ("Agreement") is hereby made between the undersigned student Contributor and Illinois Wesleyan University ("IWU").

The Contributor hereby grants IWU a perpetual non-exclusive, worldwide, royalty-free License to use, display, distribute, transmit, publish, reproduce, or copy the Content, either digitally, in print, or in any other medium. For purposes of this Agreement, Content means the audio, visual, textual, graphical, or other materials provided by the Contributor under this Agreement as identified in Attachment A. Other than the License granted herein, the Contributor retains all intellectual property rights to the Content and the responsibility for enforcing those rights. The Contributor retains the right to revoke the non-exclusive license granted hereunder upon written notice to IWU. Upon receipt of such written notice, IWU will, within ninety (90) days, cease and desists from using the Content.

The Contributor represents and warrants that to the best of his/her knowledge: (i) he/she is the sole owner of the Content or has been otherwise authorized by the owner of the Content to use the Content as contemplated herein, and has secured all necessary licenses, consents, and authorizations with respect to use of Content and all elements thereof to the full extent contemplated herein; and (ii) no part of the Content violates or infringes upon the patent rights, copyrights, trade secrets, trademarks, or constitutes defamation, invasion of privacy or the violation of any right of publicity or other rights of any person or entity. If the Content contains any material which is not original, then the Contributor must: (a) must provide IWU written permission from the copyright holder of said material; or (b) remove the material form the Content.

The Contributor specifically acknowledges that the Content may constitute an educational record under FERPA (20 U.S.C. § 1232g) and expressly consents to the use of the Content as contemplated under this Agreement.

This Agreement contains the entire agreement and understanding between the Contributor and IWU with respect to the subject matter hereof and merges all prior discussions and representations with respect to the subject matter of this Agreement. No amendment or modification hereof shall be valid or binding upon the parties unless made in writing and signed by all parties. This Agreement shall be governed by and construed under applicable federal law and the laws of the State of Illinois, and the parties expressly agree that jurisdiction and venue of any dispute shall exclusively be in McLean County, Illinois.

Contributor Information:

Name: ______________________________

Signature: ______________________________ Date: ____________

Address: ______________________________

City: ____________________ State: ________ Zip Code: ________

Phone: ______________________________

Email: ______________________________

Attachment A. Identification of Content

Title of Content: ______________________________

Author(s): ______________________________

Date Content was Created: ______________________________

Description of Content: ______________________________

____

____

____

For more information contact:

Karen Schmidt University Librarian
Illinois Wesleyan University
Ames Library Bloomington, Illinois 61701
309-556-3834
karens@iwu.edu

Lawrence University

Policies for Lux

Introduction

Lux is the digital home for the scholarly and creative works of the Lawrence University community. Lux brings these resources together in one place to collect, preserve, and provide long-term access to them. This is an evolving repository whose scope may change over time.

Collection

Examples of content:

- Annual Report
- Article
- Conference Proceeding
- Honors Project
- Oral History
- Senior Experience

Adding Content

Members of the Lawrence community interested in submitting materials should consult with the Lux coordinator at lux@lawrence.edu. Appropriate content may be added following the guidelines below:

1. The work must be original, produced and submitted, or sponsored by a faculty, staff, student, organization, or department of Lawrence University.
2. The work must be creative, scholarly in nature, research-oriented, or of institutional significance.
3. The author must own the copyright to all components and content within the work, or have received and show permission to have the material available in Lux.
4. The author or representative of the organization or department must sign a permission form prior to material being available online, granting Lawrence the right to distribute and preserve the material via Lux.
5. At the discretion of the author, material may be available only on the Lawrence University campus.
6. There is no formal limit to the size of material.
7. Most file formats are acceptable.

Author Rights

1. The author retains the copyright for all works submitted.
2. The author is free to reuse the content, but it is his/her responsibility to check the terms of the publication agreement if a document published in Lux is published elsewhere.

User Rights

1. All users must respect the intellectual property rights of the author.
2. Material may be downloaded for educational and research purposes provided due recognition is given to the author.
3. Material may not be copied, distributed, displayed, altered, or used for commercial purposes unless specified by Creative Commons License (http://creativecommons.org/).
4. If you have questions about permitted uses for any content in this database, please email us (lux@lawrence.edu).

Withdrawal of Content

Lux is a permanent repository. Once deposited, an item will not typically be withdrawn unless removal is legally required.

Preservation and Format Support Policy

The Library will use standard data management practices to protect the items stored in Lux. The database will be backed up regularly and will be kept secure against unauthorized deletion or modification.

Lux can accept many file formats. The long-term preservation of the complete and original functionality of certain file formats, however, may not be practical or possible. Digital files depend on the availability of the appropriate software to render the functions and appearance intended by the file's creator; over time, older software applications may no longer function on new computer platforms, leaving the files created with those applications inoperable. The level of access that the Library can assure to items stored in Lux may therefore range from preservation of the full functionality and appearance of the original file to the preservation of only the bit stream with no assurance that the file's original functionality or appearance can be recreated.

In general, files created with open or non-proprietary software offer the greatest likelihood that their functionality and appearance can continue to be rendered as computer environments change. Creators of digital content are urged to carefully consider the implications of choosing one or another file format or software application and to balance the importance of the functions provided by a software application against the importance of being able to preserve those functions over a period of years or decades.

A table of file formats can be found here: http://lux.lawrence.edu/file_types.pdf. It is recommended that those depositing content in Lux use formats in the left-hand column if at all possible, and consider methods for converting files with low probability to formats with higher probability.

Frequently Asked Questions

I don't have electronic versions of old working papers that I'd like to include in the repository. Is it okay to scan the printed page to a PDF file?

Yes. Scanning printed pages is a great way to create PDF files for inclusion in the repository. There are two ways to scan a page: using OCR (Optical Character Recognition) or scanning the page as an image. Making OCR scans requires careful proofreading and loses the original formatting of the documents. Image scans cannot be searched. The best solution takes advantage of both of these methods. Many software applications allow for the OCR capture of image scans. When documents are scanned this way, users see the image scan but can search the full text of the document. This is the preferred method for scanning documents for the repository.

When I copy and paste abstracts into the Submit form, some formatted text reverts to plain text. What's going on?

When copying abstracts from a word processing file or a PDF file and pasting the text into the submission form, you are taking text from an environment that supports fonts and text style changes. Because the abstract is intended to be presented on the web, text styles must be specified using HTML codes.

If submitting an abstract in HTML format, please be sure to select the corresponding option on the submission form.

The following HTML tags are recognized by the system and may be used to format an abstract (use lowercase tags):

<p>—paragraph	
<p>This is the first paragraph.</p> <p>This is the second paragraph.</p>	This is the first paragraph. This is the second paragraph.
** —line break**	
<p>This is a line of text with a linebreak here. This is text after</p>	This is a line of text with a linebreak here. This is text after
<strong>—strong/bold	
<strong>bold text</strong>	**bold text**
<em>—italics/emphasis	
<em>italicized text</em>	*italicized text*

<sub>—subscript	
Text with <**sub**>subscript</**sub**>	Text with $_{\text{subscript}}$
<sup>—superscript	
Text with <**sup**>superscript</**sup**>	Text with ^{superscript}

How do I include accents and special characters in the abstracts and titles?
The repository software supports the worldwide character set (Unicode, utf-8). Accents, symbols, and other special characters may be copied and pasted into the abstract or title field from a word processing file or typed in directly. Windows users may also use the **Character Map** to insert these characters. Macintosh users may use the **Character Palette** (available via **Edit** > **Special Characters** in the Finder).

How do I revise a submission?
To revise a submission that has been posted to the repository, contact the repository administrator with the new version. Please note that Honors Projects are loaded in their final form and cannot be revised.

If the submission has been submitted, but not yet posted, you may revise it via your **My Account** page:

Locate the article on your **My Account** page and click the title. Click **Revise Submission** from the list of options in the left sidebar. Enter your changes in the Revise Submission form and click **Submit** at the bottom of the page to submit your changes. (You only need to modify the portion of the form that corresponds to the changes you wish to make.)

How can I submit a multi-part file, such as multiple chapters for a book?
Combine all the sections together into one Microsoft Word file or PDF file and submit that. To make one PDF file from multiple files, open the first PDF file, then choose **Document > Insert Pages** from Acrobat's menus to insert the second file (indicate it should go after the last page of the first file) and repeat for all documents. The result will be one compound PDF file which may then be submitted.

If you feel that the one large PDF file might be too large for some people to download, we suggest that you submit the consolidated file as the full text of the article and then upload the separate chapters or sections of the document as **Associated Files**. These files will appear on the web page alongside the complete document. For more information about uploading associated files, see **below**.

Can I post related files (sound clips, data sets, etc.) alongside the published article?
Yes. The bepress system refers to these supplementary items as **Associated Files**. You will be prompted to submit Associated Files when you upload your submissions. The name of the files you

upload will appear on the website along with your short description of it. Viewers must have the necessary software to open your files; that is, not provided by the bepress system. Please be sure that there are no permissions issues related to use of the associated material. Sometimes, especially with images, you must write a letter seeking permission to use the material before it can be posted.

Also note that where possible, items such as images, charts, and tables that are referenced in the document (or otherwise an integral part of the document) should be included directly in the article itself and not posted just as associated files.

Can I post a reprint from a journal?
It depends on what the journal allows, which is usually specified in their agreement with the author. If it would not violate copyright to post the reprint on your repository site, you're welcome to do so. Permissions for many publishers can be found at **SHERPA RoMEO**.

A working paper in our repository site has been published in a slightly revised form in a journal. What should I do?
Many journals do not have any restrictions on working papers that preceded an article, especially if substantial revisions were made. You should check your author agreement with the journal to confirm that there is no problem with leaving the working paper on the site. The repository would constitute noncommercial use.

Assuming the working paper does remain on posted in the repository, it is a good idea to include the citation to the published article on the cover page of the repository working paper. Please contact the repository administrator to request this change.

Pacific University

Collection Management Policy

About CommonKnowledge

CommonKnowledge (http://commons.pacificu.edu/) is the online digital repository for the collected scholarship and creative works of Pacific University faculty, staff and students—and of their collaborators from around the world. These collections, organized and made accessible by the Pacific University Libraries, demonstrate Pacific's commitment to the idea that shared information and academic collaboration are essential to the "progress of knowledge" in our global community.

The creation and maintenance of collections in CommonKnowledge are guided by these values:

- Increasing the impact of local knowledge. The intellectual inquiry and creative expression of Pacific's faculty, staff, and students often result in work that has the potential to benefit people outside of the university.
- Promoting discovery, innovation, and interdisciplinary work. CommonKnowledge provides a way for members of the Pacific community to not only share with those within their disciplines but to also allow their work to be discovered and used in new and unanticipated ways.
- Preserving the availability of local knowledge. CommonKnowledge provides a persistent, long-term home for work created at Pacific University. By contributing their work to CommonKnowledge, students, faculty, and staff can be assured that their documents and files will be preserved and will be persistently available.

Relationship to other Digital Collections

The Pacific University Libraries maintains separate platforms for the curation of digital collections in different units. The nature and potential use of specific digital content will determine which unit should manage that content, and on which platform it should be housed:

- Digital content which falls within the collection parameters (http://www.pacificu.edu/libraries/services/scholarly-communication/common-knowledge/collection-management-policy/collection-parameters) described in this policy will be housed and managed in CommonKnowledge.
- Digital content that is determined to possess predominantly historical value, or which is properly considered to constitute a primary archival resource, will be housed and managed by the University Archives.

- Administrative records and documents from Pacific University offices and academic units will generally be deemed to fall outside of the scope of the CommonKnowledge collections; such content will be considered for inclusion in the University Archives.

Scope of Policy

This policy describes the relationship between CommonKnowledge and other digital collections held by the Pacific University Libraries, outlines the collection parameters and priorities for CommonKnowledge, and provides guidelines for the administration of those collections.

Specific processes and workflows for the administration of CommonKnowledge are not included in this document.

Although University Libraries-published journals and monographs are accessible through the CommonKnowledge platform, such works are not considered part of the repository collections. Policies governing the creation, editorial oversight, and production of University Libraries-published journals and monographs are outside the scope of this document.

Policy Revisions

This policy is reviewed by the Scholarly Communications & Research Services Librarian on an annual basis. Proposed policy revisions will be reviewed by the Local Collections and Publication Services team; final approval is provided by the University Librarian.

Acknowledgments

Some portions of content in this policy were adapted from: University of Utah IR collection policy; MIT Libraries DSpace policies, Coventry University, BioMed Central, IDEALS and OxyScholar.

Collection Parameters

Scope of Content

CommonKnowledge primarily collects scholarly and creative work created by Pacific University faculty, staff, and students. "Scholarly" work may include formal publications, gray literature (research posters, conference papers, academic papers, white papers, technical reports, program evaluations, etc.), data or databases, or any other work, irrespective of format,* which is of potential value to scholars and practitioners in any discipline. "Creative" work may include artistic and literary creations, computer code (software, applications, etc.), or any other work, irrespective of format,* which is a creative expression of an individual's disciplinary skill or knowledge.

* Subject to the format guidelines outlined in this policy.

Non-Pacific Contributors

Scholarly and creative work created by individuals outside of the Pacific University community will be considered for inclusion only if the Requirements for External Contributors (https://www.pacificu.edu/libraries/services/scholarly-communication/common-knowledge/collection-management-policy/collection-parameters%23external) are satisfied.

Collection Dates

CommonKnowledge primarily serves as a mechanism for collecting the scholarly and creative work of faculty, staff, and students created during such individuals' period of employment or study at Pacific University. While employed at Pacific University, faculty members and staff may also request the inclusion of work completed prior to their arrival at the University. However, in general, scholarly and creative work created prior to 1950 will be considered of historical interest and will not be included in CommonKnowledge (see Relationship to other Digital Collections, http://www.pacificu.edu/libraries/services/scholarly-communication/common-knowledge/collection-management-policy).

Open Access

CommonKnowledge is an open access digital repository. By default, all content will be visible to public users. Except in certain circumstances (see Access Restrictions, http://www.pacificu.edu/libraries/services/scholarly-communication/common-knowledge/collection-management-policy/access-restrictions), both the metadata record for an individual item and the full-text (i.e., complete digital content) will be accessible to all users.

Content in CommonKnowledge is deemed "open access" because it is openly available and free for personal use (as permitted by U.S. copyright law). Content is not required to be distributed under a Creative Commons license.

File Formats: General

CommonKnowledge is open to scholarly and creative work in any digital format. Any type of file can be made available for download, including but not limited to: documents, audio files, video files, image files, data sets, presentation slides, and computer code. The following restrictions should be noted:

- Full-text indexing of submitted works for the native CommonKnowledge search function is available only for those works in Microsoft Word (.doc or .docx) or Adobe PDF (.pdf) format (the latter only if it is text-readable or able to have optical character recognition performed).
- There is currently no formal limitation on the size of files accepted into/distributed through CommonKnowledge; however, contributors are encouraged to limit file size to two (2)

gigabytes. Files which would prove difficult for users to efficiently download over slower internet connections may be compressed and made available as a .zip file.

- There is currently limited support for streaming media in CommonKnowledge. If a contributor wishes a media file (audio or video) to be streamed in CommonKnowledge, the file must be hosted by the contributor (on a personal or institutional server, YouTube, or Vimeo), and the link provided as part of the CommonKnowledge deposit.
- Future format migration will be performed as necessary/as possible. While there are no guarantees as to the persistent integrity of digital file formats, reasonable efforts will be made to maintain the integrity of .doc/.docx, .pdf, .html, .xml, .gif, .jpeg, .tiff, .aiff, .wav, .mp3, .avi, .mpeg, and .mp4 files (see Preservation, http://www.lib.pacificu.edu/ck-preservation/, for further information).

File Formats: Accessibility

The University Libraries are committed to making digital content in CommonKnowledge accessible to individuals with disabilities. Individuals contributing content to CommonKnowledge should ensure that their files comply with federal accessibility guidelines. Guidelines for individual files types (Microsoft Office Suite, Adobe Acrobat, HTML, and multimedia files) are available at hhs.gov (http://www.hhs.gov/web/508/accessiblefiles/index.html).

Collection Priorities

Content recruitment and resource allocation for support and administration of collections will be determined by the CommonKnowledge collection priorities (in descending order):

Level 1 Priorities

- Theses, dissertations, and other culminating projects (both undergraduate and graduate)
    - ✧ Exemplary student academic work (other than culminating projects)
    - ✧ Student publications*
    - ✧ Faculty publications†
    - ✧ Collaborative student/faculty publications or academic work
    - ✧ Faculty gray literature
    - ✧ Open educational resources

Level 2 Priorities

- Materials from scholarly conferences held at, or sponsored by, Pacific University
- Collections composed primarily of content from external contributors (subject to Requirements for External Contributors, https://www.pacificu.edu/libraries/services/

* Pre-prints, post-prints, or published versions.
† Pre-prints, post-prints, or published versions.

scholarly-communication/common-knowledge/collection-management-policy/collection-parameters%23external)
- Media files of student or faculty presentations or performances

Level 3 Priorities

- Data sets or databases
- University publications (from centers or offices) that are already openly available
- Image or other media collections created by Pacific University faculty or staff and designed for use in classroom teaching

Level 4 Priorities

- Administrative records or other documents from Pacific University offices or academic units

Approval of New Content Collections

CommonKnowledge contains standard collections for (a) student and (b) faculty work (publications, gray literature, or other general academic work) from each college, school, or other academic unit. There are also standard collections for culminating student projects (theses, dissertations, capstone projects, etc.) from each college or school, as appropriate.

Additional collections for specific types of content may be created at the request of faculty, staff, or administrators. New collections can be created in any of four (4) configurations:

- **Series**: Appropriate for simple organization/dissemination of individual digital files (e.g., articles, posters, media files, etc.)
- **Monograph**: Appropriate for organization/dissemination of compound objects (e.g., books with multiple chapters, editions, or translations; or primary objects with multiple supplementary files)
- **Image Gallery**: Appropriate for organization/dissemination of digital images
- **Conference**: Appropriate for academic/scholarly meetings, conferences, and events

Proposed content for collections must be consistent with the CommonKnowledge collection parameters and priorities outlined in this document. Proposed collections are also subject to the guidelines in "Eligibility to Contribute" and "Requirements for External Contributors" below.

All new collection requests will be reviewed by the Scholarly Communications & Research Services Librarian and may be subject to the approval of the University Librarian. Collection requests that do not meet the requirements of this policy may be granted in exceptional circumstances and as resources allow.

Eligibility to Contribute

All current Pacific University students, faculty,* and staff are eligible to contribute to CommonKnowledge during their course of study or employment at the University (subject to the parameters of individual content collections, which are determined either by the University Libraries or the collection administrators, as appropriate; see Content Administration, http://www.pacificu.edu/libraries/services/scholarly-communication/common-knowledge/collection-management-policy/content-administration). Faculty and staff may contribute content created prior to their employment at Pacific University.

Pacific University alumni are also eligible to contribute; preference will be given for work creating during their course of study at the University.

Requirements for External Contributors

Individuals or corporate entities who do not meet the criteria described in "Eligibility to Contribute" will be considered external to Pacific University. External individuals or entities may

- contribute content to CommonKnowledge if at least one (1) of the following criteria is met:
    - ✧ content was created collaboratively with a current (at the time of submission) Pacific University student, staff member, or faculty member, and the Pacific collaborator(s) assents to the deposit in CommonKnowledge; or
    - ✧ content was created for an academic/scholarly meeting, conference, or event hosted or sponsored by Pacific University, and for which there is an existing conference structure in CommonKnowledge;
    - ✧ content was commissioned, distributed, or published by a Pacific University office or academic unit; or
    - ✧ content is added as part of an approved collection created at the request of an external corporate entity.

External corporate entities may (b) request the creation of new content collections in CommonKnowledge if *all* the following criteria are met:

- at least one (1) Pacific University staff member or faculty member is currently affiliated (in an official capacity, such as membership or holding office) with the corporate entity; and
- at least one (1) Pacific University office or academic unit agrees to co-sponsor the content collection with the external entity; and
- the external entity and Pacific University sponsor agree to enter into a memorandum of understanding with the University Libraries regarding the administration of the content collection, which shall include a provision for continual affiliation with Pacific University.

All proposed contributions and content collections from external individuals or corporate entities must be consistent with the CommonKnowledge collection parameters and priorities outlined in this document.

* Adjunct faculty members must have a minimum of (1) academic year total service to the University to be eligible.

Content Administration

Selection and Submission

The Scholarly Communications & Research Services Librarian, as well as the Local Collections and Publication Services team, and the other liaison librarians within the University Libraries, are all responsible for (a) communicating the purpose of CommonKnowledge to faculty, staff, and students, and (b) identifying and recruiting content for inclusion in CommonKnowledge.

Content may be submitted to CommonKnowledge directly by contributors or by library staff on behalf of contributors. Submission by contributors requires the creation of a personal account within CommonKnowledge.

Submitted content is routed into a mediated publication queue; content will not be posted to CommonKnowledge until the following is verified:

- The contributor is eligible (see Eligibility to Contribute, http://www.pacificu.edu/libraries/services/scholarly-communication/common-knowledge/collection-management-policy/collection-parameters%23eligibility, and Requirements for External Contributors, http://www.pacificu.edu/libraries/services/scholarly-communication/common-knowledge/collection-management-policy/collection-parameters%23external).
- The content has been submitted to the appropriate collection.
- All metadata required for the specific collection has been supplied.
- The contributor has completed the CommonKnowledge submission agreement (as part of the online submission process for direct submissions, or as a separate document for mediated submissions).
- The file(s) supplied is the correct version, is not corrupted/unreadable, and (in the case of previously published work) does not violate publishers' posting policies.

Editorial Responsibility

CommonKnowledge is open to eligible scholarly and creative work, whether or not that work has undergone external peer-review prior to submission.

The University Libraries do not provide editorial support or facilitate peer review for content in the repository. Individuals submitting work to CommonKnowledge, whether through an online submission form or through an administrator-mediated submission, are solely responsible for the content of their work. While the University Libraries reserve the right to request assurances or relevant documentation from submitting authors related to the legality of their submissions (and to delay posting until said assurances or documentation are received), CommonKnowledge administrators do not systematically review the content of submissions for compliance with intellectual property, privacy, or other applicable law.

Though works from University Libraries-published journals are accessible through the CommonKnowledge platform, content submitted to a journal is subject solely to the editorial and peer review policies of that journal and is not received or administered through the same workflows as content submitted for inclusion in repository collections.

Content Management

Excluding editorial oversight (other than determining that submitted content complies with the CommonKnowledge collection parameters and policies), the Scholarly Communications & Research Services Librarian is responsible for managing content in CommonKnowledge. Core content management responsibilities are:

- creating and configuring standard content collections, as well as any collections requested and approved by the Pacific University community or its collaborators;
- managing the creation and consistent application of relevant metadata to improve discovery and access of content collections;
- facilitating the submission and posting process for content collections (with the exception of those addressed in "Independent Content Management" below);
- obtaining and preserving appropriate license agreements from contributors;
- maintaining the integrity of the "version of record" for individual works included in CommonKnowledge (consistent with Corrections and Withdrawals, http://www.pacificu.edu/libraries/services/scholarly-communication/common-knowledge/collection-management-policy/corrections-withdrawals);
- determining appropriate access restrictions, if any, for individual works or content collections, and ensuring that such restrictions are correctly applied;
- making determinations on requests to withdraw individual works or collections from CommonKnowledge (consistent with Corrections and Withdrawals, http://www.pacificu.edu/libraries/services/scholarly-communication/common-knowledge/collection-management-policy/corrections-withdrawals);
- performing an appraisal of long-term preservation needs within twenty (20) years of the creation of each content collection; and
- communicating with the Pacific University community, and especially with content contributors, regarding updates or changes to the CommonKnowledge platform or policies that will affect the access or presentation of their content.

Independent Content Management

Although the Scholarly Communication & Research Services Librarian is ultimately responsible for the administration of content in CommonKnowledge, limited content management functions may be delegated to other individuals for specific collections, particularly for those collections developed in partnership with an external entity or collections where independent editorial oversight is required.

Requests for independent management of new or existing content collections will generally be approved in the following circumstances:

- The content in the collection is subject to the review/approval (prior to public posting) of the academic unit, office, or external entity from which the content was produced.
- The content in the collection requires substantive editorial oversight and/or revision prior to public posting.

- The collection is connected to an event (e.g., academic conference) and requires oversight by the organizing individual(s) or body.
- The content in the collection otherwise requires management or oversight beyond the scope of that provided by the Scholarly Communication & Research Services Librarian.

Individuals, academic units, offices, or external entities that assume independent management of a content collection are responsible for

- collaborating with the Scholarly Communication & Research Services Librarian to develop consistent standards for the submission and description of content in the collection;
- ensuring that content posted in the collection complies with copyright and other intellectual property laws;
- ensuring that content posted in the collection does not violate any individual's or entity's rights (especially privacy rights);
- ensuring that content posted, and the administration of that content, complies with all applicable parts of this policy; and
- promptly reporting any technical errors or issues with the content collection to the Scholarly Communication & Research Services Librarian.

Individuals, academic units, offices, or external entities that assume independent management of a content collection retain the right to

- determine who is eligible to submit content to the collection;
- determine what type of content is eligible for submission;
- determine the appropriate access restrictions (if any) for content;
- correct or withdraw content; and
- receive a copy of all metadata and digital files from the collection within (2) weeks of such a request.

Note: All of these rights must be exercised within the bounds of, and consistent with, this policy.

For content collections under independent management, the University Libraries retain the right to

- refuse or de-accession content that is not within the CommonKnowledge collection scope, or that otherwise violates this policy;
- assume management of collections for which the independent manager(s) is not meeting the responsibilities outlined in this policy;
- distribute/redistribute metadata for all content to improve access or visibility of content;
- migrate content locations and formats as needed;
- set limits of content size and type, or determine an appropriate fee-for-service, if a collection requires the allocation of additional Library resources (system, financial, or human) to appropriately manage; and
- perform an appraisal for long-term archiving when new content is not added to a collection for a period of one (1) year or more or within twenty (20) years of the creation of a collection, whichever comes first.

For content collections under independent management, the University Libraries commits to

- notify collection manager(s) of significant changes to either content (e.g., format migration) or system (e.g., system upgrades or outages); and
- return content to collection managers if the Libraries cease to support CommonKnowledge.

Metadata

Descriptive Metadata

A basic descriptive metadata record is required for all content contributed to CommonKnowledge. Required elements are:

- Title
- Creator(s)
- Date (Publication or Creation)
- Rights

Additional recommended elements are:

- Description
- Subject(s)

All metadata elements are coded by the system using the Dublin Core metadata elements (elements with an asterisk are automatically assigned by the system but may be used for additional custom metadata fields):

- dc:title
- dc:creator
- dc:description
- dc:date
- dc:type*
- dc:format*
- dc:identifier*
- dc:source*
- dc:publisher*
- dc:subject

Although the basic elements of title, creator, date, and rights are required, custom field display labels may be created for each collection within CommonKnowledge. There is no limit on the number of custom metadata fields (beyond the required elements) that may be created for individual collections.

Subject Headings

The default controlled vocabulary for subject headings used in CommonKnowledge is the Discipline taxonomy provided by the Digital Commons system. It is recommended that a minimum of (1) discipline term be assigned for each item contributed to CommonKnowledge.

In addition to the Discipline taxonomy, custom fields may be created for individual series if another controlled vocabulary is required (e.g., Library of Congress Subject Headings, Medical Subject Headings, etc.).

Name Authority

Only one accepted name format will be used for each individual listed in the Creator metadata field of an item record in CommonKnowledge. The same name must be used for all item records in which that individual is listed as a Creator.

For Pacific University-affiliated individuals, the accepted name will be that used in conjunction with the individual's Pacific University network account, unless a variant name is requested in writing by the individual in question.

For non-Pacific University-affiliated individuals, the accepted name will be that used in the initial metadata submitted to CommonKnowledge by the individual in question (or by an individual submitting on his/her behalf). Requests to use a variant name must be made in writing.

Institutional Affiliation

All individuals submitting work to CommonKnowledge are encouraged, though not required, to include an institutional affiliation along with their preferred name.

For Pacific University faculty, staff, and students, the institutional affiliation must be "Pacific University". Departmental affiliations, if desired, must be reflected in a separate field (e.g., Comments). For content that was created by faculty or staff before their employment at Pacific University, pre-Pacific institutional affiliations will not be recorded as part of the individual's name/affiliation metadata. (It may be reflected in a separate field)

For external contributors, the institutional affiliation at the time of submission to CommonKnowledge should be used.

Recommended Citations

A recommended citation for each item in CommonKnowledge is generated by Digital Commons. This recommended citation may be revised within an individual content collection to adhere to a specific citation style (e.g., APA, MLA, Chicago, etc.). The same citation style must be used across an individual content collection.

User Commenting

Commenting Functionality

An optional reader commenting plug-in may be added to a content collection at the request of the department/unit/school/office that provides the content for the collection.

Reader comments on CommonKnowledge content are not initially moderated; readers may post comments after creating an account (which requires provision of an email address) through the plug-in. However, all posted comments will be reviewed by the Scholarly Communications and Research Services Librarian according to the policy below. (Comment moderation/review will not be delegated, even for independently managed content collections.)

Comment Moderation Policy*

The University Libraries reserve the right to remove a comment at any time if the comment

- is indecent, offensive, or contains negative content of a personal, racial, ethnic, sexual orientation, or religious character—or otherwise appears to be libelous or violate the privacy of any individual or corporate body; or
- purports to provide medical or legal advice and does not cite published literature as the basis for the statements therein; or
- is irrelevant to the article or is otherwise trivial; or
- appears to be advertising a product or service; or
- is not in English (resources for confirming the content of non-English comments are not available); or
- is otherwise deemed inappropriate.

Preservation

Content Standards

It is recommended that for text-based content, files be submitted to CommonKnowledge in the PDF/A format. Other recommend formats include: .pdf, .doc/.docx, .html, and .xml. For multimedia-based content, the recommended file formats for submissions are: .gif, .jpeg, .tiff., .aiff, .wav, .mp3, .avi, .mpeg, and .mp4.

While there are no guarantees as to the persistent integrity of digital file formats, the University Libraries will make reasonable efforts to maintain the integrity of .doc/.docx, .pdf, .html, and xml files. Content submitted to CommonKnowledge in formats other than those listed will be considered for preservation efforts on a case-by-case basis, as resources allow.

---

* Adapted from BioMed Central

Format Migration

University Libraries

Every ten (10) years, the support for/utility of the file formats list above will be assessed by the University Libraries. As necessary (and as possible), content in formats for which viewers/readers are becoming rare in common use will be migrated to new formats with broader support. (New formats that are experimental or lack an established user community will not be used without careful evaluation).

Outside of the ten-year file format review cycle, individual files/content may be migrated if its determined that the original files have become corrupted or unstable.

Berkeley Electronic Press

The Digital Commons system preserves all objects uploaded to the repository in their original format. This provides the ability to build in capabilities for either emulation (provision of a virtual environment that can display a digital object in its native format), or migration. Beyond this, Berkeley Electronic Press (bepress) is committed to making PDFs web accessible on a permanent basis. If Adobe changes Acrobat to such an extent that older PDFs are no longer readable, bepress will migrate these objects to ensure they remain readable.

Backup

On a quarterly basis, the University Libraries will receive a delivery of all CommonKnowledge metadata and associated files via FTP or SFTP from bepress. The previous two (2) quarterly deliveries will be stored securely on a rolling basis on a local or virtual server, as well as on a hard drive, by the University Libraries.

System Migration or Termination

If the University Libraries ceases its Digital Commons license, bepress will provide a final content delivery upon license expiration to allow migration to a new repository platform.

If the University Libraries ceases to support CommonKnowledge (as distinct from migrating CommonKnowledge to a new platform), all content will be transferred to the Pacific University Archives and to individual units/offices/schools/departments that request copies of content they (or their faculty/students/staff) have provided.

Content Policies

All contributors to CommonKnowledge are required to complete a formal submission agreement (or provide analogous assurances in writing) that describes the disposition of intellectual property within the submitted work, and which acknowledges the contributors' responsibilities with regard to the content of the submission. Depending on the configuration of the specific content collection, the submission agreement will be completed either physically, via email, or via the CommonKnowledge platform.

Copyright

Contributors to CommonKnowledge must hold the copyright (either solely or jointly) or have the permission of the copyright holder(s) (with the exceptions noted below) for the content that they submit to CommonKnowledge. Copyright for content submitted to CommonKnowledge is retained by the author/creator/copyright holder(s); no copyrights are transferred to Pacific University or the University Libraries. However, contributors must provide Pacific University and the University Libraries with a non-exclusive, royalty-free license to use, display, distribute, transmit, copy, reproduce, archive or otherwise make accessible the content through CommonKnowledge.

Inclusion of Third-Party Copyrighted Materials / Fair Use

For previously published full-text materials (e.g., journal articles), the copyright status of each item will be reviewed prior to public posting in CommonKnowledge, and every effort will be made to ensure that ingesting and providing access through CommonKnowledge is in compliance with copyright holders' stated policies.

For unpublished materials (e.g., student coursework, theses/dissertations, faculty or student conference presentations, etc.) assurances will be received from the creator(s) during the submission process that, if necessary, permission has been obtained from owners of third-party copyrighted materials included in the unpublished work. In the instance of a mediated submission wherein a formal submission agreement is not received, it is assumed that the creator of the work is not knowingly submitting infringing material.

The University Libraries do not review for compliance with copyright law the content of all such scholarly or creative unpublished materials that are submitted to CommonKnowledge. Furthermore, the libraries fully support the right of our community members to make fair use of copyrighted materials (as outlined in Title 17, Section 107 of the U.S. Code) in the creation of their own works. The Scholarly Communications and Research Services Librarian will not make a fair use determination of submitted work; such a determination is considered to be the responsibility of the creator(s). However, in instances when it is readily and reasonably apparent that copyright law would be violated by posting a work, the University Libraries may request that the creator(s) obtain permission from any relevant copyright holder(s).

Collaborative Works

The University Libraries encourages submission of collaborative works to CommonKnowledge. When works with multiple authors, creators, or owners are submitted for inclusion in CommonKnowledge, the submitting author or owner is responsible for ensuring that the submission does not violate any existing contractual agreements governing the work and that the submission conforms to all applicable policies and laws.

Under United States copyright law, individual authors in a joint work share equal rights in that work (absent a contract to the contrary) and, as such, have the right to independently grant a non-exclusive license like that required by CommonKnowledge. Given this, the University Libraries do not require that all co-authors provide permission to post a work in CommonKnowledge. However, it is recommended that the submitting author consult with his or her co-authors prior to submitting a work to CommonKnowledge.

- Exception: *All* student authors must grant permission for a shared work to be submitted to CommonKnowledge. Permission may either be granted explicitly or may be attested to by the submitting author.

Terms of Use

The following terms govern third-party use of content contributed to CommonKnowledge:

General Terms of Use

For previously published works (journal articles, book chapters, etc.) for which the publisher retains copyright, permission has been granted (where necessary) to post this Material on CommonKnowledge. For any use which exceeds personal use or fair use, permission may be required by the copyright owner of the Material (see "Comments" section in the Material record).

For theses, dissertations, or other previously unpublished scholarly or creative works, the right to download or print any portion of this Material is granted by the copyright owner only for personal or educational use. The author/creator retains all proprietary rights, including copyright ownership. Any editing, other reproduction, or other use of this Material by any means requires the express written permission of the copyright owner.

Except as provided above, or for any other use that is allowed by fair use (Title 17, §107 U.S.C.), you may not reproduce, republish, post, transmit, or distribute any Material from this website in any physical or digital form without the permission of the copyright owner of the Material.

Inquiries regarding further use of these materials should be addressed to: CommonKnowledge Rights, Pacific University Library, 2043 College Way, Forest Grove, OR 97116, (503) 352-7209. Email inquiries may be directed to: copyright@pacificu.edu.

Terms of Use for Creative Commons-Licensed Works

For works posted in CommonKnowledge that display a Creative Commons license in their record and/or on the work itself, the use of that work is governed by the terms of the license selected by the content creator.

For more information about Creative Commons licenses, or to license your own work, please visit http://creativecommons.org/.

Take-Down Policy

To assure compliance with the Digital Millennium Copyright Act, the University Libraries have instituted the following policy to address claims of copyright infringement in works contributed to CommonKnowledge:

Persons who have questions, or who believe that their copyrights have been infringed upon by the posting of material to CommonKnowledge, may contact the administrators at:

CommonKnowledge Rights, Pacific University Library, 2043 College Way, Forest Grove, OR 97116, (503) 352-7209. Email inquiries may be directed to: copyright@pacificu.edu.

Requests to remove materials from CommonKnowledge should include

1. a physical or electronic signature of the owner, or authorized agent of the owner, of an exclusive right that is allegedly infringed;
2. clear identification of the copyrighted work(s) claimed to have been infringed;
3. clear identification of the material in CommonKnowledge that is claimed to be infringing, including the URL(s);
4. information reasonably sufficient to permit the University Libraries to contact the complaining party, such as an address, telephone number, and, if available, an electronic mail address at which the complaining party may be contacted;
5. a statement that the complaining party has a good faith belief that use of the material in the manner complained of is not authorized by the copyright owner, its agent, or the law; and
6. a statement that the information in the notification is accurate, and, if applicable, that the complaining party is authorized to act on behalf of the owner of an exclusive right that is allegedly infringed.

The University Libraries will respond to all questions or requests within one business day. If within that timeframe the libraries are not able to determine that the use of the work in question is lawful, access to the work through CommonKnowledge will be removed.

Privacy

No works that infringe on an individual's privacy rights under law or under the Pacific University Privacy Policy may be submitted for inclusion in CommonKnowledge. Upon notification that content in CommonKnowledge (a) infringes on an individual's privacy rights under the law, (b) is in violation of the Pacific University Privacy Policy, or (c) is in violation of FERPA, HIPAA, or other relevant privacy laws, the Scholarly Communications and Research Services Librarian will, in consultation with the contributor, immediately withdraw or amend said content in a manner consistent with the procedures outlined in this policy (see Corrections and Withdrawals, http://www.pacificu.edu/libraries/services/scholarly-communication/common-knowledge/collection-management-policy/corrections-withdrawals).

Defamation*

The University Libraries fully support the intellectual and academic freedom of the faculty, staff, and students within the Pacific University community. However, the libraries also recognize that those freedoms may only be exercised to the extent that they do not become unlawful. As such, the libraries require that contributors to CommonKnowledge refrain from statements that would be considered defamatory in a court of law.

As with the use of third-party copyright materials, the University Libraries will not review content submitted to CommonKnowledge for the inclusion of potentially defamatory material. However, if material of a defamatory nature comes to the attention of the University Libraries, such material may be removed from CommonKnowledge without notice.

Any individual who believes that content in CommonKnowledge may be defamatory of them or others must inform the Scholarly Communications and Research Services Librarian as soon as possible. Defamation claims may be submitted to: CommonKnowledge—Defamation Claims, Pacific University Library, 2043 College Way, Forest Grove, OR, 97115, (503) 352-7209. Email inquiries may be directed to: gilmani@pacificu.edu.

Claims of defamation should include

1. a physical or electronic signature of the individual claiming defamation (of self or others);
2. clear identification of the content in CommonKnowledge which is believed to contain defamatory statements, including the URLS(s);
3. a clear description of the defamatory statements, as well as the rationale for the defamation claim;
4. information reasonably sufficient to permit the University Libraries to contact the complaining party, such as an address, telephone number, and, if available, an electronic mail address at which the complaining party may be contacted.

Upon receipt of a defamation claim, the Scholarly Communications and Research Services Librarian will disable access to the content in question and will consult with Pacific University's legal counsel regarding the merits of the claim. If, after this consultation, the content is determined not to be defamatory, access may be restored.

The University Libraries, pending consultation with legal counsel, may also remove potentially defamatory content which comes to light independently apart from this claims/complaint procedure.

Human Subject Research

Unpublished products (e.g., manuscripts, posters, datasets, etc.) of human subjects research will only be accepted for inclusion in CommonKnowledge under the following conditions: (a) the

* Adapted from Coventry University.

associated research study was approved by the Pacific University Institutional Review Board;[†] (b) the distribution of research results through the repository is consistent with the nature of dissemination described to research subjects in the study's informed consent document; (c) the distribution of research results through the repository has been approved by study sponsors/funders; and (d) appropriate measures consistent with the study's protocol have been taken to ensure that distribution of results through the repository does not place subjects' privacy at additional risk. The University Libraries reserve the right to confirm approval of associated studies with the Institutional Review Board prior to making submitted research products accessible.

Datasets and Databases

All data products derived from (a) human subject research, (b) private educational records, (c) private health records, or (d) any other data source that is considered private by law must comply with the following guidelines prior to deposit in CommonKnowledge:

1. Appropriate consent and/or authorization for the collection/use of the data that does not include language that would prohibit the data from being distributed through the repository must have been obtained by the depositor.
2. As appropriate, given the terms of said consent and/or authorization, all direct identifiers must have been removed prior to deposit. For data covered by the Health Insurance Portability and Accountability Act (HIPAA) Privacy Rule, all eighteen identifiers must be removed (unless appropriate authorization has been granted for other forms of disclosure).

The University Library reserves the right to request documentation of appropriate consent and/or authorization for use of the data prior to making submitted data products accessible. Data derived from human subject research studies are also subject to the conditions of deposit for such studies described elsewhere in this policy.

Access Restrictions

By default, all content in CommonKnowledge will be visible and fully accessible to public users—this includes both the metadata record and the full text (i.e., complete digital content) for individual items. However, in certain circumstances, it may be necessary or appropriate to place access restrictions on individual items or content collections. For example, a publisher may require an embargo of six to twelve months before making a journal article publicly accessible.

Access restrictions in CommonKnowledge may be requested during the submission process by an individual contributor or by the academic unit, office, or external entity from which a content collection was produced. Access restrictions requested by student contributors must be approved by their school, program, or department, as appropriate. The University Libraries may also impose

† For research products that are the result of collaborative research and for which ethical oversight has been ceded to another institution's IRB, the approval of that IRB shall be sufficient. Products of international research collaborations for which ethical oversight has been provided in another country will be accepted for deposit upon the assurance of ethical review by an IRB or relevant analogous body.

access restrictions on content in response to concerns about unlawful or unethical content (see Content Policies, https://www.pacificu.edu/libraries/services/scholarly-communication/commonknowledge/collection-management-policy/content-policies). Access may be restricted either at the individual item level or at the collection level.

There are currently three levels of access restrictions available for content in CommonKnowledge:

- **On-campus access:** The full text of content may be downloaded only from a computer within the IP range of a Pacific University campus. This can include off-campus access via a proxy server.
- **Closed access:** The full text of content is embargoed (i.e., accessible to no one) for a specific period of time (either six, twelve, or twenty-four months), but the metadata record is publicly visible.
- **Dark access:** Content is submitted to CommonKnowledge but is not publicly posted (i.e., public metadata record is created). This option is available only in cases where legal or personal safety issues are present. Dark access may be temporary or maintained indefinitely.

On-campus access and closed access are available both for individual items and for entire content collections; dark access is available only for individual items. It is important to note that the on-campus access option must be configured at the collection level, which means that no content in that collection will be visible in the Digital Commons Network (though it will still be indexed by search engines)—even individual items within the collection that have been set to open access.

Changing Access Levels

If an individual contributor or academic unit, office, or external entity for which a content collection was produced wishes to change the access level for an item or collection, such a request must be made in writing to the Scholarly Communications and Research Services Librarian.

Renewing Access Restrictions

If an access restriction on an item or collection has been set for a specific period of time, the access level will automatically revert to open access at the expiration of the restricted period, unless the Scholarly Communications and Research Services Librarian is notified in writing at least 48 hours in advance by the individual or group who contributed the content in question. The contributing individual or group is responsible for renewing a temporary restriction; no reminders will be sent by the University Libraries prior to the time period lapsing.

Corrections and Withdrawals

CommonKnowledge is intended to provide persistent access to scholarly and creative works—to serve as an authoritative record of each work's provenance and to maintain a reliable version of record for each work. As such, items contributed to CommonKnowledge should be considered permanent additions to the scholarly record. However, in some instances, it may be appropriate to provide access to a corrected version of a work or to withdraw a work from CommonKnowledge. The options for correction or withdrawal will vary upon the nature of the work and the unique circumstances of the request for such action.

Corrections or Retractions of Published Works

In order to ensure that all users who access scholarly articles (pre-prints, post-prints, or published PDFs) through CommonKnowledge have an avenue to be apprised of corrections or retractions made by the article's publisher, the DOI, or other persistent identifier that links to the article on the publisher's website will be provided within the metadata for each article posted in CommonKnowledge.

If the University Library is notified of a correction or retraction to a published article, an appropriate prominent notation will be made in the CommonKnowledge record and a link to the notice of correction or retraction provided within the metadata for that article. If possible for corrected articles, an updated version of the article will be posted and access to the original version will be maintained as a supplemental file. For retracted articles, access to the original version will be maintained but a watermark will be added to the document to indicate its retraction by the publisher.

Correction or Withdrawal of Unpublished Works

Corrections and Revised Editions

In general, corrections to unpublished works* contributed to CommonKnowledge will only be permitted if the error(s) for which the correction is requested by the author(s) seriously affect the scholarly record (e.g., if accuracy/intended meaning, scientific reproducibility, or author reputation is judged to be compromised). Errors in an unpublished work that do not affect the contribution in a material way (e.g., minor grammatical or typographical errors that do not affect the meaning of the work), and that were not introduced by the University Libraries in the process of posting the work to CommonKnowledge, will usually not be corrected. In instances where a correction is made to a work, the corrected work will be made available as the primary download but an errata note will be added to the metadata record that describes that nature of the correction and the date the corrected work became available. The original version of the work will be retained within CommonKnowledge but will not be visible or accessible to users.

---

* This does not include pre-prints or post-prints of works that were published in a final form elsewhere; providing a link in the CommonKnowledge metadata record to the final published work is considered sufficient. Corrections or retractions of the final published article will be addressed as described in the previous section.

In some cases, a contributor may request that a revised edition of a posted work be made available. A revised edition of a work distinguished from a corrected work in that new or updated content is added to the original work for a purpose other than correcting an error. For example, an author may add new content to an open textbook or open educational resource. In such cases, the revised edition of the work may either (a) replace the original edition but with access to the original edition retained as a supplemental file, or (b) be uploaded as a new item with a distinct metadata record that includes an appropriate version statement and a link back to the original/previous edition. In the latter instance, the metadata record (and potentially cover/title page) for the original/previous edition will be amended to include a prominent link to the newer edition.

Requests for corrections or uploading of a revised edition of a work should be made to the Scholarly Communications and Research Services Librarian.

Withdrawals

In order to preserve the integrity and accuracy of the scholarly record, works contributed to CommonKnowledge will only be withdrawn under limited circumstances. Such circumstances include notification by an author, contributor, or other affected party that a work: (a) contains factual inaccuracies, (b) contains plagiarism, (c) infringes on copyright or any other intellectual property right, (d) infringes on an individual or corporate privacy right, or (e) includes defamatory statements. [Note: Works will not be withdrawn if the contributing author (i.e., faculty or staff member) leaves the employ of Pacific University. (In such cases, updated contact information may be added to the record, but the item metadata and access will not be changed.)]

Any request for withdrawal must be made to the Scholarly Communications and Research Services Librarian. Requests based on claims of copyright infringement will be subject to the CommonKnowledge Take-Down Policy (http://www.pacificu.edu/libraries/services/scholarly-communication/common-knowledge/collection-management-policy/content-policies%23takedown); requests based on claims of defamation will be handled as described in the Defamation (http://www.pacificu.edu/libraries/services/scholarly-communication/common-knowledge/collection-management-policy/content-policies%23defamation) section. All other requests are subject to the following procedures:

- Requests for withdrawal may be made by authors or contributors of the work in question, or by any other affected party.
- Request must be made in writing.
- Pending a final determination, full-text access to the work in question will be temporarily disabled for all users.
- No content will be permanently removed from CommonKnowledge without an attempt to reach the author.
- All determinations as to permanent withdrawal will be made within ten (10) working days of the initial request.

If it is determined that a work should be withdrawn from CommonKnowledge, full-text access to that work will be removed permanently for all users. However, in order to preserve the scholarly record—and because the withdrawn work may have been cited using the CommonKnowledge URL—a metadata "tombstone" will be maintained at the original URL. This will include the original metadata for the work as well as a note in the record that describes the purpose for the withdrawal: either "Removed at author's request," "Removed at Pacific University Libraries' discretion," or "Removed by legal order." This metadata record will be visible but will be removed from further indexing by web search engines and made unavailable for metadata harvesting.

Pacific University

CommonKnowledge Copyright Policies

Rights and Terms of Use for Material Posted in CommonKnowledge

These terms of use apply to any works without a Creative Commons license (see below).

For **previously published** works (journal articles, book chapters, etc.) for which the publisher retains copyright, permission has been granted (where necessary) to post this Material on CommonKnowledge. For any use which exceeds personal use or fair use, permission may be required by the copyright owner of the Material (see "Comments" section in the Material record).

For **theses, dissertations, or other previously unpublished scholarly or creative works**, the right to download or print any portion of this Material is granted by the copyright owner only for personal or educational use. The author/creator retains all proprietary rights, including copyright ownership. Any editing, other reproduction, or other use of this Material by any means requires the express written permission of the copyright owner.

Except as provided above, or for any other use that is allowed by fair use (Title 17, §107 U.S.C.), you may not reproduce, republish, post, transmit, or distribute any Material from this website in any physical or digital form without the permission of the copyright owner of the Material.

Inquiries regarding further use of these materials should be addressed to: CommonKnowledge Rights, Pacific University Library, 2043 College Way, Forest Grove, OR 97116, (503) 352-7209. Email inquiries may be directed to: copyright@pacificu.edu.

Creative Commons-Licensed Works Posted in CommonKnowledge

For works posted in CommonKnowledge that display a Creative Commons license in their record and/or on the work itself, the use of that work is governed by the terms of the license selected by the content creator.

For more information about Creative Commons licenses, or to license your own work, please visit http://creativecommons.org/.

CommonKnowledge Take-Down Policy

For **previously published full-text materials** (e.g., journal articles), the University Library reviews the copyright status of each item, and every effort is made to ensure that ingesting and providing access through CommonKnowledge is in compliance with copyright holders' stated policies.

For **unpublished materials** (e.g., student coursework, theses/dissertations, faculty or student conference presentations, etc.), assurances are received from the creator(s) during the submission process that, if necessary, permission has been obtained from owners of third-party copyrighted materials included in the unpublished work. In the instance of a mediated submission wherein a formal submission agreement is not received, it is assumed that the creator of the work is not knowingly submitting infringing material.

The University Library does not review for compliance with copyright law the content of all such scholarly or creative unpublished materials that are submitted to CommonKnowledge. Furthermore, the Library fully supports the right of our community members to make fair use of copyrighted materials (as outlined in Section 107 of Title 17 U.S. Code) in the creation of their own works. CommonKnowledge administrators will not make a fair use determination of submitted work; such a determination is considered to be the responsibility of the creator(s). However, in instances when it is readily and reasonably apparent that copyright law would be violated by posting a work, CommonKnowledge administrators may request that the creator(s) obtain permission from any relevant copyright holder(s).

Take-Down Requests

Persons who have questions, or who believe that their copyrights have been infringed upon by the posting of material to CommonKnowledge, may contact the administrators at: CommonKnowledge Rights, Pacific University Library, 2043 College Way, Forest Grove, OR 97116, (503) 352-7209. Email inquiries may be directed to: copyright@pacificu.edu.

Requests to remove materials from CommonKnowledge should include

1. a physical or electronic signature of the owner, or authorized agent of the owner, of an exclusive right that is allegedly infringed;
2. clear identification of the copyrighted work(s) claimed to have been infringed;
3. clear identification of the material in CommonKnowledge that is claimed to be infringing, including the URL(s);
4. information reasonably sufficient to permit the University Library to contact the complaining party, such as an address, telephone number, and, if available, an electronic mail address at which the complaining party may be contacted;
5. a statement that the complaining party has a good faith belief that use of the material in the manner complained of is not authorized by the copyright owner, its agent, or the law; and
6. a statement that the information in the notification is accurate, and if applicable, that the complaining party is authorized to act on behalf of the owner of an exclusive right that is allegedly infringed.

The University Library will respond to all questions or requests within one business day. If within that timeframe the Library is not able to determine that the use of the work in question is lawful, access to the work through CommonKnowledge will be removed.

Touro College and University System

Institutional Repository Policies and Procedures

Mission Statement

Touro Scholar is an online institutional repository supporting the research and teaching mission of Touro College and University System (including New York Medical College). It is intended to both preserve and promote the research and scholarship of the Touro community to the wider public. The Touro Libraries maintain this repository.

Access Policy

The repository is intended as an open access resource to Touro research and scholarship. This means that most material on the repository will be freely available to the public. Some material may not immediately be freely available due to publisher embargoes, copyright, or other issues. Some access is restricted to Touro College and University System member use.

Content Policy

Content is restricted to works that fall within the faculty, staff, or student's scope of research, scholarship, creative work being conducted, or field of study being pursued at the Touro College and University System. Campus policies on materials accepted are subject to change.

Examples of eligible material include:

- abstracts published in scholarly/academic journals
- conference/symposium articles in published proceedings
- articles in scholarly/academic/professional journals
- published books (authored/edited)
- published book chapters (authored/edited)
- published book/film reviews in academic publications
- creative works—curated or published; not self-published (poetry, novels, short stories, published plays, art exhibits, musical scores and choreographed dance, audiovisuals)
- published encyclopedia entries (excluding Wikipedia)
- letters to the editor, if published in peer-reviewed journals
- data sets and other supplements for published materials

- student works submitted by department heads, such as
    - master's theses
    - capstone papers
    - poster presentations
    - doctoral dissertations
- department-published journals
- poster presentations
- presentation slides from conferences or professional organization meetings (i.e., APTA Combined Sections Meeting)
- doctoral dissertations
- campus-specific submissions (see appendix)

Submission Policy

Current Touro College and University System faculty, staff, and students with faculty sponsorship (meaning that their work has been approved by a faculty member) may only submit work which they have authored or co-authored, and which they have a legal right to submit. Depositors must not submit materials with confidential information and must have permission from all co-authors. Full texts of publications must be deposited, although there may be a delay in making the publication publicly visible to comply with publishers' embargoes or other issues. Authors/depositors take the responsibility for the integrity and usability of the data, not Touro College and University System. Any intellectual property rights violations are entirely the responsibility of the authors/depositors; administrators only vet materials for depositor eligibility, mission relevance, format, and exclusion of spam. Materials that violate these rules will be removed.

In order to manage submissions most efficiently, we request that units appoint contacts who will collaborate with the libraries in depositing the material.

Author Rights

The "pre-print" refers to the author's copy before it has been submitted for peer review. The "post-print" is the author's copy after it has undergone and incorporated peer review but before it has been formatted, etc. by the publisher. The "definitive version" would be the publisher's PDF—the version of the article after it has been peer-reviewed and formatted by the publisher. This is the version that will actually appear in the publication. We will accept pre-prints only if the article has already been published—if this is the only copy the depositor has access to. We do not accept pre-prints of articles that have not been published.

Pre-print: The author retains the right

- to post a pre-print version of the article on a public electronic server connected to the world wide web;

- to post a pre-print or reprint of the article on an internal or external server controlled exclusively by the author or employer, provided that such posting is noncommercial in nature and the article is made available to users without a fee or a charge and if the following statement appears on first page or screen of the paper as posted on the server: *This article was (will be) published in <> [insert name of publication] and is made available as an electronic reprint (pre-print) with permission of the publisher. One print or electronic copy may be made for personal use only. Systematic or multiple reproduction, distribution to multiple locations via electronic or other means, duplication of any material in this paper for a fee or commercial purposes, or modification of content of the article are prohibited*;
- to post and update the article on non-publisher servers (including e-print servers) as long as access to such servers is not for commercial use and does not depend on payment of access, subscription, or membership fees; any such posting made or updated after acceptance of the article for publication shall include the citation information and copyright notice, and should provide an electronic link to the journal's website.

Post-print: The author retains the right

- to self-archive an author-created version of his/her article on his/her own website and his/her institution's repository, including his/her final version; however, the author may not use the publisher's PDF version which is posted on <> without permission; the author may only post his/her version provided acknowledgement is given to the original source of publication and a link is inserted to the published article on the publisher's web site; the link must be accompanied by the following text: *"the original publication is available at < >" [insert URL where brackets are]*;
- to post and update the article on e-print servers as long as files prepared and/or formatted by the publisher or its vendors are not used for that purpose unless permission has been obtained; any such posting made or updated after acceptance of the article for publication shall include a link to the online abstract in the publisher's journal of to the entry page of the journal;
- upload the author's accepted manuscript PDF ("post-print") to institutional and/or centrally organized repositories but must stipulate that public availability be delayed until <> *[insert appropriate numbers of months]* months after first online publication in the journal.
- When uploading an accepted manuscript to a repository, the author should include a credit line and a link to the final published version of the article. This will guarantee that the definitive version is readily available to those accessing your article from public repositories and means that the article is more likely to be cited correctly: *This is a pre-copy-editing, author-produced PDF of an article accepted for publication in [insert journal title] following peer review. The definitive publisher-authenticated version [insert complete citation information here] is available online at: <> [insert URL that the author will receive upon publication here]*.

Definitive version: The author retains the right

- to post an electronic version of the final publisher's file of the article on the author's current institutional internet server for limited non-commercial distribution, provided that proper notice of the publisher's copyright is included and that no separate or additional fees are collected for access to or distribution of the article apart from the internet access fees which may be paid to an internet access provider.

Student work:
When a category of work from a campus will be included on Touro Scholar (for example, all theses from a specific campus' school) citations will be included minimally for the works of all students. Students may restrict or not provide rights to full-text access for a certain amount of time. Students will be required to provide an abstract and keywords for posting and to provide some access.

Preservation Policy

Materials will be retained indefinitely, with emphasis put on continued accessibility; however, it may not be possible for certain files to continue to be readable if they are in unusual formats.

Materials may not normally be removed from the repository but may be for certain reasons, for example, if publishers' rules mandate it or there is a proven violation of copyright. Once an item has been deposited, it may not be changed. Errata/corrigenda may be included and, if absolutely necessary, an updated version of the material may be submitted.

Style Guide

Manuscript format: Articles submitted must conform to the following guidelines to be considered for publication, and not following them may result in materials being sent back to depositors for revision.

Materials must include at a minimum:

- author(s) names
- Touro department/school
- title of article or book
- name of journal, volume, issue, or date
- page numbers (if not online-only journals or article number if online-only and available)
- DOI if available; if not, URL of the article if available
- abstract—the abstract should be factual in nature and include both the purpose and the major conclusions of the article (This is a short summary and should not contain references. If the author does not include an abstract, the administrators may write one instead. Administrators may also edit abstracts.)
- keywords—authors are requested to provide keywords that relate to the article or book (Administrators will also assign keywords if the author does not provide them, and/or add additional terms if the author does provide keywords.)

- file format—it is preferred that files be submitted in .pdf form; if manuscripts are submitted in Microsoft Word or Rich Text Format (.rtf), please turn off the "track changes" feature
- persistent identifier—not required but strongly suggested is including the depositor ResearcherID, Scopus, or ORCID

Author's Deposit Agreement

(Adapted from University of Michigan's Agreement and Marquette University Graduate School Publishing Document)

I hereby grant to Touro College and University System the non-exclusive right to retain, reproduce, and distribute the deposited work(s) (the Work(s)), in whole or in part, in and from its (their) electronic format. This agreement does not represent a transfer of copyright to Touro College and University System.

Touro College and University System may make and keep more than one copy of the Work(s) for purposes of security, backup, preservation, and access, and may migrate the Work(s) to any medium or format for the purpose of preservation and access in the future. Touro College and University System will not make any alteration, other than as allowed by this agreement, to the Work(s).

I represent and warrant to Touro College and University System that the Work(s) is (are) my original work. I also represent that the Work(s) does (do) not, to the best of my knowledge, infringe or violate any rights of others. For quoted material, including, but not limited to, text, images, and graphs, I believe such usage falls within fair use or I have obtained permission for use. I understand that any copyright violation is mine and that Touro College and University System shall be held harmless.

I further represent and warrant that I have obtained all necessary rights to permit the Touro College and University System to reproduce and distribute the Work(s) and that any third-party-owned content is clearly identified and acknowledged within the Work(s).

By granting this license, I acknowledge that I have read and agreed to the terms of this agreement and all related policies.

Appendix: Campus-Specific Submissions

New York Medical College

- Historical medical instruments
- Digitized yearbooks
- NYMC newsletters
- Campus historical material

Touro University California

- Campus historical material
- Departmental newsletters or journals
- Digitized yearbooks

Touro University Nevada
Touro College of Osteopathic Medicine—New York
Touro College of Osteopathic Medicine—Middletown
Touro College of Pharmacy—New York

University of Nebraska-Lincoln

Publisher Permission Letter

Permissions Department / Managing Editor / Editor / etc.

Dear […],

I am working with **Dr.** ____________________________ of the University of Nebraska-Lincoln to deposit electronic versions of her papers in the University of Nebraska-Lincoln's institutional repository < http://digitalcommons.unl.edu > for educational and research purposes.

I am writing to request permission to deposit an electronic version of the following article from ____________________________:
[citation]

This request is for non-exclusive, non-commercial, one-time, single-use permission for this purpose ("educational and research") only. Copyright notice, citation of original publication data, DOI number, and a hotlink to your site (if desired) will be given.

Our repository is the institutional archive, maintained at the University Library, for research and scholarship emanating from the University of Nebraska-Lincoln. A single electronic version will be archived and become available for viewing by visitors to the Library's Digital Commons site. For more information about the repository or its policies, please contact me at the email or phone below.

May we have permission to deposit an electronic version of this article?

Thank you for your assistance.

Paul Royster
Scholarly Communication
306 Love Library
University of Nebraska-Lincoln
402 472-3628
proyster@unl.edu
http://digitalcommons.unl.edu

University of South Florida

Professor Permission Letter

Dear Professor [last name],

Research universities throughout the world are committed to increasing access to the scholarly output of their faculty and students. Individual researchers are similarly interested in promoting their work as widely as possible while preserving copyright and intellectual property ownership. In response, web-accessible collections of published research are emerging in many universities and research institutions. These "Institutional Repositories" (IR) offer open access to a range of research, including published peer-reviewed articles, preprints, presentations, data, and more.

This spring, the USF Tampa Library is launching **Scholar Commons** (http://scholarcommons.usf.edu/), USF's institutional repository, to serve our research community. Following a scan of departments across campus, we have identified three that can serve as the best candidates for a pilot project that we will conduct in the coming months. A high percentage of your department's faculty have published research in journals that support IRs by providing blanket permission to upload the papers into the resource.

What are the benefits of Scholar Commons?

- Scholar Commons offers powerful dissemination that compliments traditional publishing and expedites immediate access to your scholarly work.
- Scholar Commons asserts copyright ownership and allows you to freely and legally link to your research output.
- Scholar Commons satisfy requirements to publicly disseminate the results of grant-generated research.
- Scholar Commons' platform is optimized for visibility through Google and other search engines, resulting in being more frequently cited, more visible, and receiving greater impact.
- Scholar Commons provides the global community barrier- and cost-free access to your important research. In a time when the average annual scholarly journal subscription costs $1,200, open access is more important than ever before.
- Scholar Commons provides participating faculty a monthly "readership report" with download statistics.
- Scholar Commons is archived and digitally preserved against future vendor service interruptions.

What are we asking you to do in our pilot? **Nothing!** If you are willing to allow the USF Tampa Library to include the works listed in the attached document in the Scholar Commons repository pilot, *no action is required.* We will do all of the work to make the material accessible to the global audience. If you do not wish to allow us to include your work in the repository, please notify me by April 1, 2011. If you have questions or concerns, please feel free to send those to me.

Because you are part of a pilot project, you can expect enhancements as the project expands. Although we will communicate information about enhancements as it is available, additional details about the pilot and the Scholar Commons service are included in the attached document.

Thank you for your consideration,

Todd Chavez
Director, Academic Resources
USF Libraries
tchavez@usf.edu

This form was developed by the University of South Florida and is included here by permission.

Valparaiso University

Digital Scholarship, Publishing, Preservation

Content Submission Policies and Guidelines

Introduction

ValpoScholar, a service of the Christopher Center Library and the Valparaiso University Law Library, is a digital repository and publication platform designed to collect, preserve, and make accessible the scholarly output of Valparaiso University (Valpo) faculty, students, staff, and affiliates.

This document outlines policies and guidelines regarding the submission of content to ValpoScholar, including submission criteria, author and user rights, and procedures for removing posted content.

Submission Criteria

To best represent the spectrum of Valparaiso University scholarly work, ValpoScholar maintains an inclusive collection policy based on the principle of Open Access (OA), which emphasizes broad electronic dissemination of scholarly works. Members of the Valpo community interested in submitting materials should review the policies and guidelines below prior to submission. Please contact a ValpoScholar administrator for questions or clarifications. Appropriate content may be added following the guidelines below:

- The work must be original, produced and submitted, or sponsored by a faculty, staff, student, organization, or department of Valparaiso University.
- The work must be creative, scholarly in nature, research-oriented, or of institutional significance.
- The author must own the copyright to all components and content within the work or have received and shown permission to have the material available in ValpoScholar.
- The author or representative of the organization or department must sign a release form prior to material being uploaded to the repository granting Valparaiso University the right to distribute and preserve the material via ValpoScholar.
- Content submitted by students will require the approval of a faculty mentor or sponsor involved in the creation of the work.
- Contributors may include non-affiliated scholars if they are co-authoring with Valpo authors, are affiliated closely with the university, or are submitting via a Valpo-sponsored publication, conference, or event.

- Although most content is open access, some material may be available only to current university faculty, staff, and students, or may be the subject of a publishing embargo for a fixed period.
- The work must be in digital form, including supplementary materials. Ideally, all of the digital components of a submission will be provided as a set.
- A wide range of file formats is accepted (including text files, datasets, audio files, and video files) and there is no formal limit to the size of material. Examples of possible content include:
    a. journals produced by the Valparaiso University community
    b. published articles or preprints when copyright and/or license allow
    c. books or book chapters when copyright and/or license allow
    d. working papers, conference papers, and technical reports
    e. honors projects, senior theses, and other distinguished student work
    f. datasets
    g. institutional or organizational newsletters, reports, and related materials
    h. image collections or audiovisual materials, either primary or supplementary

Please note that the following content is not permitted for submission/publication to ValpoScholar:

- FERPA-protected information, including student email addresses;
- HIPAA-regulated information (protected health information), including any information related to the past, present, or future physical or mental health of an individual, except only if the individual has authorized release of his or her information in writing, and such release is in the hands of the publisher;
- content barred by law or regulation from publication;
- intellectual property for which the submitter does not have permission to submit and distribute;
- non-public personally identifiable financial or contact information of any kind, including, but not limited to, social security numbers, credit/debit card numbers, account numbers, account balances, and private residential addresses, except only where such records preexist as legitimate publicly accessible records outside the university;
- photographic depictions of individuals in areas where a reasonable expectation of privacy exists, except only if all individuals depicted have given written consent to publication of their image; or
- records protected by state privacy laws (please note that privacy laws vary by state, and protect their residents even when they are out of state

Author Rights

- The author retains the copyright for all works submitted.
- The author is free to reuse the content, but it is his or her responsibility to check the terms of the publication agreement if a document published in ValpoScholar is published elsewhere.

- Authors may update and add to existing works.
- Click this link for information on the Valparaiso University Copyright Policy: http://libguides.valpo.edu/copyrightinformation.

User Rights

- All users must respect the intellectual property rights of the author.
- Material may be downloaded for educational and research purposes provided due recognition is given to the author.
- Material may not be copied, distributed, displayed, altered, or used for commercial purposes unless such use is specified by a Creative Commons License.
- Click this link for information on Fair Use exceptions to copyright law: http://www.copyright.com/Services/copyrightoncampus/basics/fairuse_list.html.

Removal of Content

ValpoScholar is a permanent repository. Once deposited, an item will not be withdrawn unless removal is legally required. However, under some circumstances a work may be removed from view:

- Authors or affected parties may request that works be removed for reasons of factual inaccuracy, plagiarism, or potential copyright infringement.
- No materials will be removed without an attempt to reach the author.
- If a work is removed, a citation including original metadata will always remain, with a note regarding the removal; e.g., "removed at request of author," or "removed at the discretion of ...," or "removed by legal order."

Valparaiso University Libraries thanks Pepperdine University Libraries for permission to use the Pepperdine University Content Submission Policies and Guidelines document as the basis for this document.

Valparaiso University

*Valpo***Scholar** (http://scholar.valpo.edu)

What it is and why you should use it

Whether you are a student just completing an honors research project or a seasoned professor with a preprint of a new article, ask yourself these questions:

- Would you like to make the full text of your work easy to find online and instantly available to a broad readership in an electronic, open access environment?
- How about the peace of mind that comes with knowing that your work resides in a trusted, sustainable, and fully accessible digital repository?
- Perhaps you're the editor of a print-based journal—how would you like to reach a new global readership online while maintaining your journal's branded look and identity?

These are just some of the services provided by ValpoScholar, the university's centralized exchange for Valparaiso University (Valpo) journals, faculty web pages, conference proceedings, exemplary student research, and other forms of scholarship. ValpoScholar, a service of the Christopher Center Library and the Valparaiso University Law Library, is a digital repository and publication platform designed to collect, preserve, and make accessible the academic output of Valpo faculty, students, staff, and affiliates.

Some Advantages of ValpoScholar

- Items in ValpoScholar are search engine optimized, meaning that they appear high in the search results of sites like Google and Google Scholar.
- Authors and editors receive regular download reports.
- ValpoScholar provides workflows for peer-review publishing, conference management, and individual scholar sites.
- ValpoScholar can support multimedia materials, including datasets, audio files, and video.

Requesting SelectedWorks: Faculty Publication Pages

The Valpo SelectedWorks Author Gallery allows Valpo faculty to create their own search engine optimized website in minutes, submit papers directly to the ValpoScholar repository, and build a network of colleagues who follow their work. Each SelectedWorks author page provides a fully searchable gallery of that author's academic work with full-text downloads of each item available to site visitors.

Some advantages of SelectedWorks

- SelectedWorks gives faculty control of their online presence and ensures that their work is collected together in one place and gets into the hands of interested colleagues.
- Readers can sign up for email alerts and RSS feeds for any scholar page to be notified of updates and new work.
- Content uploaded to SelectedWorks sites is indexed in Google web search and Google Scholar for maximum discoverability and impact. SelectedWorks sites quickly become one of the top results for online searches of the scholar's name.
- Regular readership reports allow administrators and faculty to track how many people are viewing and downloading their work, and who has signed up for their email alerts.
- As with any ValpoScholar service, authors retain full copyright to their submitted works.

How to request and build your own SelectedWorks page

- Go to the Berkeley Electronic Press website (http://works.bepress.com).
- Create a free bepress account to log in.
- Follow the step-by-step instructions in the Site Builder.
- For assistance with building your SelectedWorks site, please contact Jonathan Bull (jon.bull@valpo.edu).

Requesting Journal Hosting

ValpoScholar provides an online, open access, or subscription-based publishing platform for Valpo-based or affiliated journals. Open access publishing in association with institutional repositories, such as ValpoScholar, has emerged as a viable alternative to commercial publishing and represents the vanguard of scholarly communication. More than a simple repository, ValpoScholar includes journal management software to manage the entire editorial process online in a streamlined, efficient, and purely electronic manner. Editors can easily customize workflows, control their journal settings and policies, and manage the submission process online. The built-in peer-review module simplifies and expedites the peer-review process by tracking submission and referee activity, automatically emailing appropriate reminders, and providing a mechanism for anonymous correspondence between reviewer and author. Furthermore, web design options in ValpoScholar allow your journal to maintain its branded look or identity, including cover art. For examples, browse Valpo journals currently in ValpoScholar.

ValpoScholar Journal Hosting Policies

For those interested in starting a new journal in ValpoScholar, please review the following policies and procedures and contact Jonathan Bull (jon.bull@valpo.edu) to begin the setup procedure.

1. **Journals are encouraged to be open access compliant.** Although subscription-based journals are a possibility in ValpoScholar, our goal is to provide open access for all journals that are published in the repository. Therefore, priority support will be given for journals that are open access immediately upon publication. Library staff will work with departments that seek to have a subscription-based journal only if they are willing to consider a two-year or less embargo. (In other words, provide open access to back issues after no more than two years after publication.)
2. **Journals should be considered ongoing in nature.** In order to ensure the sustainability of all journals, all requests must first be approved by the administrative head of the department or division from which the journal originates. Student initiatives must additionally have a dedicated faculty sponsor.
3. **Peer-reviewed journals should have an editorial board.** An editorial board should be designated to serve as the body overseeing the editorial policies and to manage the peer-review procedures. If the editorial board is comprised of students, at least one faculty member must be on the editorial board to help ensure continuity.
4. **Authors retain their copyright.** All authors of individual articles retain their copyright to the works submitted; however, all submissions become a permanent part of the ValpoScholar repository. Once deposited, an article will not be withdrawn unless removal is legally required or special circumstances intervene (such as factual inaccuracy, plagiarism, or potential copyright infringement). All authors must click through an agreement statement specific to your journal that includes deposit in ValpoScholar.
5. **Journals will be assigned an ISSN.** The International Standard Serial Number (ISSN) is the unique identifier used to distinguish serials. If the journal exists currently as a print publication, a separate ISSN will be assigned for the online publication. For more information on ISSN, see www.loc.gov/issn/faq.html.
6. **Advertising and promotion is the responsibility of the publishing department or entity.** Valparaiso University Libraries are not responsible for promoting or publicizing your journal.

Procedures for requesting the start of a new journal

1. **Fill out and submit a New Journal Request Form.** All requests to start a journal in ValpoScholar must be accompanied by a completed New Journal Request Form. This form can be requested from Jonathan Bull (jon.bull@valpo.edu) and includes basic content and design information about your journal as well as information regarding the editorial staff and desired editorial workflow. This form must also be signed by a faculty sponsor.
2. **Approval of request.** All requests will be reviewed by Jonathan Bull (jon.bull@valpo.edu), Scholarly Communication Services Librarian. In order to allow sufficient time, please submit requests at least two months prior to the desired launch date for your journal.

3. **Implementation—the Library's responsibilities.** Upon approval of a request, library staff will
   - set up the journal site within ValpoScholar;
   - provide training on administering the journal site to editors;
   - submit information on the journal to the Directory of Open Access Journals: http://www.doaj.org/;
   - submit a request for an ISSN for the journal; and
   - notify cataloging when we have an ISSN in order to add the journal title to our catalog for increased discovery and access.
4. **Implementation—the journal editors' responsibilities.** Journal editors, or a similar entity representing the stewardship of the journal, or journal staff, have the following responsibilities:
   - Journal editors will approve the basic design and content of the journal's ValpoScholar site developed by the library or Berkeley Electronic Press.
   - Following training by library staff, editors or journal staff will upload present and future content (journal articles/issues) to the journal ValpoScholar site.
   - Following training by library staff, editors or journal staff will scan (as necessary) and upload preexisting journal content (journal articles/issues) to the journal ValpoScholar site.
   - Following training by library staff, editors will manage the editorial workflow for their journal, including the submission process, peer-review (if relevant), selection, revisions, communications with authors, etc.
5. **Discontinuation of a journal.** If no new content or issues are produced for two consecutive years, the journal will be considered to have "ceased publication." The ValpoScholar administrator will contact the department head or faculty sponsor and confirm that the journal is no longer being published and appropriate notices will be placed in ValpoScholar and in the catalog record.

Conference/Symposia management and posting

In addition to providing back-end management for journal publishing, ValpoScholar also provides tools for organizing and managing academic conferences or symposia and then posting the proceedings online. With the ValpoScholar management software, conference organizers have the tools to easily manage electronic paper submission, peer review, acceptance, permissions, and publication. They can post the event schedule and the embedded registration directly on the conference site. Papers and presentations from the event, including supplementary multimedia files, appear in a "series" in ValpoScholar, which are typically organized by research unit, center, or department.

For more information on using ValpoScholar to organize your next conference and publish its proceedings online, see "How to request and build a series in ValpoScholar" in the section below.

Posting working papers, preprints, datasets, student work, etc.

ValpoScholar also provides an online, open access publishing platform for Valpo-based or affiliated academic work in a variety of other contexts and formats. These include

1. published articles or preprints when copyright and/or license allow;
2. books or book chapters when copyright and/or license allow;
3. working papers, conference papers, and technical reports;
4. honors projects, senior theses, and other distinguished student work;
5. datasets; and
6. institutional or organizational newsletters, reports, and related materials.

Like conference and symposium materials, these types of works typically take the form of a series in ValpoScholar organized by research unit, center, or department.

How to request and build a series in ValpoScholar

- Please review our content submission guidelines.
- Contact Jonathan Bull (jon.bull@valpo.edu) with a series proposal or description of the work that you would like to submit to the repository. Please include the following at a minimum:
    - ✧ name of series/work: Department, academic unit, or related discipline
    - ✧ date of work(s) or event
    - ✧ name(s) of primary contact(s)
    - ✧ actual or anticipated breadth of material to upload (e.g., number of articles, presentations, papers, etc.)
    - ✧ actual or anticipated file formats (e.g., PDF, spreadsheet, audio file, etc.)
    - ✧ extent of series, such as whether it will continue to populate in the future
- If accepted, library staff will create the series and train the submitting party to upload and manage the event/materials.
- Authors participating in series hosted by ValpoScholar are asked to sign a Non-Exclusive Release Form for Use of Materials, which should be collected by the series/event organizer and submitted to Jonathan Bull (jon.bull@valpo.edu).

Valparaiso University Libraries thanks Pepperdine University Libraries for permission to adapt and use their Digital Commons informational web page.